The Elements of Social Scientific Thinking

The Elements of Social Scientific Thinking

ELEVENTH EDITION

TODD DONOVAN
Western Washington University

KENNETH HOOVER
Western Washington University

Australia • Brazil • Japan • Korea • Mexico • Singapore • Spain • United Kingdom • United States

WADSWORTH
CENGAGE Learning

The Elements of Social Scientific Thinking, **Eleventh Edition**

Todd Donovan, Kenneth Hoover

Publisher: Suzanne Jeans

Executive Editor: Carolyn Merrill

Acquisitions Editor: Anita Devine

Development Editor: Lauren Athmer, LEAP Publishing Services, Inc.

Assistant Editor: Patrick Roach

Editorial Assistant: Eireann Aspell

Media Editor: Laura Hildebrand

Executive Marketing Manager: Stacey Purviance

Brand Manager: Lydia LeStar

Senior Marketing Communications Manager: Linda Yip

Rights Acquisitions Specialist: Jennifer Meyer Dare

Manufacturing Planner: Fola Orekoya

Art and Design Direction, Production Management, and Composition: Cenveo Publisher Services

Cover Image: Rachelle Antoinette

For product information and technology assistance, contact us at
Cengage Learning Customer & Sales Support, 1-800-354-9706.

For permission to use material from this text or product, submit all requests online at **www.cengage.com/permissions**.
Further permissions questions can be emailed to **permissionrequest@cengage.com**.

Library of Congress Control Number: 2012946261

ISBN-13: 978-1-133-60767-0

ISBN-10: 1-133-60767-5

Wadsworth
20 Channel Center Street
Boston, MA, 02210
USA

Cengage Learning is a leading provider of customized learning solutions with office locations around the globe, including Singapore, the United Kingdom, Australia, Mexico, Brazil, and Japan. Locate your local office at **international.cengage.com/region**

Cengage Learning products are represented in Canada by Nelson Education, Ltd.

For your course and learning solutions, visit **www.cengage.com**.

Purchase any of our products at your local college store or at our preferred online store www.cengagebrain.com.

Instructors: Please visit **login.cengage.com** and log in to access instructor-specific resources.

Printed in the United States of America
1 2 3 4 5 6 7 16 15 14 13 12

Contents

Preface

This little book is not very complicated. It is, rather, an initiation into social science intended for those who use the results of social science research and for those taking their first steps as researchers. We tackle such fundamental questions as: Where do concepts come from? What is a variable? How do we measure things? Why bother with scientific thinking? How is a hypothesis different from other statements about reality? How is it similar?

Our intent has been to help readers see through some false images of social science and to say enough to make the first steps in research possible for them, while leaving the elaboration of the technicalities of research operations to more detailed and specialized sources. Throughout, the emphasis is on reality testing as a process by which we can know what to make of the world. This presentation of science is not a narrow one—we encourage the reader to be scientific in daily thought as well as in the specific application of social scientific methods.

Our conviction is that the debate between social scientists who quantify and those who do not (and between so-called positivists and antipositivists) has served the valuable purpose of broadening the array of tools and perspectives available to social scientists. This debate has also absorbed a huge amount of energy and enterprise that would now be better directed at making constructive use of all the techniques of social analysis. If nothing else, it is evident that no single approach holds all the answers and that every approach has its particular pitfalls and openings to prejudice. Choosing the appropriate methodology, or combination of methodologies, is the critical consideration. We do not take sides on this debate, but offer this book as a way of introducing people to basic ideas about quantitative social science.

While social scientists have been occupied with these debates, society's problems seem to have grown more complex and difficult to resolve. If careful observation is critical in understanding these problems, then social science has a key role to play.

The classic rules of scientific inquiry provide a framework for resolving conflicts over that most contentious matter, the truth, even between people who do not particularly like each other. Useful ideas from all sources of insight badly need to be tested through systematic analysis so that conflicting points of view can be resolved into productive forms of action.

CHANGES IN THE ELEVENTH EDITION

This book had its origins more than 30 years ago when Kenneth Hoover, a young political theorist, reflected upon his own education in the social sciences and tried to make sense of the key concepts and techniques so that they could be explained to new generations of undergraduates. The author was initially repelled by quantitative analysis and the scientific approach to politics. However, he came to learn how it could contribute to answering what Hanna Pitkin identifies as the theorist's most basic question: What can be done to improve the human condition—and what matters are beyond our ability to change?[1] Perhaps the longevity of the book owes something to its origins outside the field of methodology and to an interest in making the tools of social science available to students interested in social change.

This eleventh edition of *The Elements of Social Scientific Thinking* continues the partnership between Kenneth Hoover, a theorist, and Todd Donovan, a more empirically oriented social scientist. Donovan joined with Hoover on the sixth edition. This is the second revision since Ken's death in 2007, but *The*

---

1. Hanna Pitkin, *Fortune is a Woman: Gender and Politics in the Thought of Nicolo Machiavelli* (Chicago: University of Chicago Press, 1999).

Elements remains a joint project and much of it remains Ken's book. Following Ken, I keep working at situating scientific knowledge with respect to other forms of "knowing" so that students will see through some of the stereotypes that have clouded this discussion. The central lesson remains the same: Social science is about the reduction of uncertainty in a world of phenomena that are only partially knowable through observation. The point of this book is to see what observation can accomplish.

This edition continues the emphasis on straightforward explanation. Numerous minor changes have been made. The increasing sophistication of statistical tools and the pervasiveness of computers, which have increased access to these tools, have necessitated some additions to the sections on research techniques. We include two appendixes that serve as examples of research questions that may be of wide interest to sociologists, political scientists, and other social scientists. Appendix A provides an introduction to a discussion of America's declining "social capital" in order to illustrate how scholars have approached the changing relationship of community involvement and political participation. Appendix B illustrates relationships among political trust, social capital, and other forces across 24 nations.

HOW TO READ THIS BOOK

Most books are meant to be read straight through. For many readers, that will be the best approach for this book. However, the reader should be aware that each chapter surveys social scientific thinking at a different level. For that reason, there can be various points of access to the book depending on the reader's needs. The first chapter, "Thinking Scientifically," sets social science in the general context of the ways in which people try to answer questions about the world around them. Chapter Two, "The Elements of Science," develops the basic outline of the scientific method by discussing concepts, variables, measurements, hypotheses, and theory.

For those faced with the immediate task of doing or understanding research, Chapter Three, "Strategies," may be a good place to begin because it deals directly with the nuts and bolts of scientific inquiry. Chapter Four, "Refinements," presumes a basic understanding of the scientific method explained in Chapter Two and provides additional research tools. Chapter Five, "Measuring Variables and Relationships," is devoted to the art and science of measurement.

For convenience of access and review, each chapter begins with an outline of the topics covered and ends with a list of the major concepts introduced, in their order of appearance. The chapters occasionally refer to examples from the appendixes included at the end of this book. Readers will benefit from consulting the appendices when they are used as examples in a chapter.

In Appendix A, an article titled "Tuning In, Tuning Out: The Strange Disappearance of Social Capital in America," by Robert Putnam, is reprinted in condensed form. The article is cited frequently in the text; those who need a good model for generating research questions will want to consider it carefully. Appendix B consists of an article titled "Trust in Government: The United States in Comparative Perspective," by Todd Donovan, David Denemark, and Shaun Bowler. Appendix B is relevant to the section on regression analysis in Chapter Five.

We invite readers of *The Elements of Social Scientific Thinking* to share their assessments of the book. Todd Donovan can be reached at the Department of Political Science, Western Washington University, Bellingham, WA 98225, or by e-mail at Todd. Donovan@wwu.edu.

ACKNOWLEDGMENTS

A work that endures for more than three decades has, in a real sense, many authors—too many to list. We have relied upon the comments of, first of all, our students, to whom we are most grateful.

Numerous critics and colleagues have made valuable suggestions. Bob Blair of the College of Wooster in Ohio helped greatly in shaping the first edition. Over several editions, the comments of Aage Clausen, Emeritus Professor of Political Science at the Ohio State University, were crucial in maintaining the distinctive mission and tone of the book. More recently, several colleagues have provided particular insights: David Darmofal at the University of South Carolina, Drew Lanier at the University of Central Florida,

Eileen Morris at California State University (Chico), and Meredith Spencer at Bridgewater State College. To all of these, full pardon and many thanks. Judy Hoover contributed ideas to the writing and a great deal more—she and Ken are both sorely missed. Lauren Athmer has been immensely patient and helpful in bringing this eleventh edition to fruition.

About the Authors

Todd Donovan (Ph.D., University of California–Riverside) is Professor of Political Science at Western Washington University. Recent books include *State and Local Politics: Institutions and Reform* (with Christopher Mooney and Daniel Smith; Wadsworth, 2010); *Losers' Consent: Elections and Democratic Legitimacy* (with Christopher Anderson, Andre Blais, Shaun Bowler, and Ola Listhaug; Oxford, 2007); and *Reforming the Republic: Electoral Institutions for the New America* (with Shaun Bowler; 2004).

Kenneth Hoover (Ph.D., University of Wisconsin–Madison) was Professor Emeritus of Political Science at Western Washington University. His final books included *The Future of Identity* (Lanham, MD: Lexington Books, 2004); *Economics as Ideology: Keynes, Laski, Hayek and the Creation of Contemporary Politics* (Lanham, MD: Rowman & Littlefield, 2003); and Kenneth Hoover with John Miles, Vernon Johnson, and Sara Weir, *Ideology and Political Life,* 3rd ed. (Wadsworth, 2001).

1

Thinking Scientifically

Why Bother to be Systematic?

The Role of Reasoned Judgment and Opinion

The Role of Imagination, Intuition, and Custom

> Every great advance in science has issued from a
> new audacity of imagination.
> —JOHN DEWEY

The phrase "social science" in print gives rise to images of a robot in a statistics laboratory reducing human activity to bloodless digits and simplified formulas. Research reports filled with mechanical-sounding words such as *empirical*, *quantitative*, *operational*, *inverse*, and *correlation* are not very poetic. Yet the stereotypes of social science created by these images are, as we will try to show, wrong.

Like any other mode of knowing, social science can be used for perverse ends; however, it can also be used for humane personal understanding. By testing thoughts against observations of reality, science helps liberate inquiry from bias, prejudice, and just plain muddle-headedness. So it is unwise to be put off by simple stereotypes—too many people accept these stereotypes and deny themselves the power of social scientific understanding.

The word **science** stands for a very great deal in our culture—some even see science as the rival of religion in the modern age. Our objective is not to examine the tangle of issues associated with science;

it is to find a path into the scientific way of thinking about things. In order to find that path, we begin by allowing some descriptions of science to emerge out of contrasts with other forms of knowledge.

First, we have to identify some distractions that should be ignored. Science is sometimes confused with **technology**, which is the application of science to various tasks. Schoolbooks that caption pictures of the latest advances in medicine with the title "Science Marches On!" aid such confusion. The technology that makes such research possible emerged from the use of scientific strategies in the study of botany, physics, bioengineering, and numerous other fields. It is the mode of inquiry that is scientific; the CT scanner is a piece of technology.

Just as science is not technology, neither is it some specific body of knowledge. For example, the popular phrase "Science tells us that smoking can kill you" really misleads. "Science" does not tell us anything; people tell us things—in this case, people who have used scientific strategies to investigate the relationship between smoking and cancer. Science as a way of thought and investigation is best conceived of as existing not in books, machinery, or reports containing numbers but rather in that invisible world of the mind. Science has to do with the way in which questions are formulated and answered; it is a set of rules and forms for inquiry and observation created by people who want verifiable answers.

Another distraction comes from identifying particular people as "scientists." That usage is not false because the people so labeled practice the scientific form of inquiry. However, is it fully honest to say that some people are scientists whereas others are nonscientists. Some people specialize in scientific approaches to knowledge, but we are all participants in the scientific way of thinking. Science is a mode of inquiry that is common to all human beings.

In becoming more conscious of your own habits of thought, you will find that there is a bit of the scientist in each of us. We measure, compare, modify beliefs, and acquire a kind of savvy about evidence in the daily business of figuring out what to do next and how to relate to others. The simplest of games involves the testing of tactics and strategies against the data of performance, and that is crudely scientific. Even trying out different styles of dress for their impact on others has an element of science in it.

The scientific way of thought is one of a number of strategies by which we try to cope with a vital reality: the uncertainty of life.

We do not know what the consequences of many of our actions will be. We may have little idea of the forces that affect us subtly or directly, gradually or suddenly. In trying to accomplish even the simplest task, such as figuring out what to eat, we do elementary calculations of what might taste good or what might be good for us. If there is enough uncertainty on that score, a little advance testing is a good idea: The queen has her taster, and the rest of us—at least when it comes to a certain hamburger—have the assurance that billions have already been sold.

Science is a process of thinking and asking questions. It is one of several ways of claiming that we know something. In one sense, the scientific method is a set of criteria for deciding how conflicts about differing views of reality can be resolved. It offers a strategy that researchers can use when approaching a question. It offers consumers of research the ability to critically assess how evidence has been developed and used in reaching a conclusion.

For Example

Social Science as a Process of Asking and Answering Questions

For ages people have asked, why do nations go to war? The question has been answered in several different ways. For some, war might be seen as a fundamental part of the human condition. Similarly, we might answer the question by claiming that there is "evil" in the world that precipitates war. Wars thus amount to "good" nations defending themselves against "bad" ones. One obvious problem with this view is that opposing sides likely each see the other as the "bad" one. Likewise, how do we measure good versus bad? Others stress the role that the nations' leaders play. Leaders who, accurately or not, think that they are more powerful than an adversary may launch an attack. Still others note that an array of factors both internal and external to a country determine whether or not a nation goes to war.

A social scientific approach to the question involves making claims about the causes of war that can be tested by multiple observations. One might examine some history of international relations to assess how leaders perceived the strength of their adversaries and then use those observations to explain why leaders launched wars when they do. Another ambitious approach involves collecting hundreds of years of data on all interactions between nations and using the data to predict when wars will and will not occur. This sort of work requires that even more questions be asked and answered systematically. What, for example, is a nation? What level of conflict between nations counts as a war?

SOURCES: John Stoessinger, *Why Nations Go to War*, 11th ed. (Cengage, 2011); Correlates of War project at http://www.correlatesofwar.org/

The scientific approach has many competitors in the search for understanding. For many people throughout most of history, the competitors have prevailed. Analysis of reality has usually been much less popular than myths, conspiracy theories, superstitions, and hunches, which have the reassuring feel of certainty *before* the event they try to predict or control, though seldom afterward. Certainly personal beliefs are a vital part of our lives. The point is that the refusal to analyze is crippling, and the skilled analyst is in a position of strength.

WHY BOTHER TO BE SYSTEMATIC?

Most human communication takes place among small groups of people who share a common language, much common experience, and an understanding of the world they live in. There is a ready-made arena for mutual agreement. Not so in a more complex social environment. Although families can transmit wisdom across generations by handing down stories and maxims, societies run into trouble. In its most cynical form, the question is, whose story is to be believed? The need to understand what is happening around us and to share experiences with others makes systematic thought and inquiry essential.

Because society is interesting for the drama it contains, there is a tendency to dispense with systematic understanding and to get on with the descriptions, stories, and personal judgments. Although these can be illuminating, they often have limited usefulness because highly subjective accounts of life form a poor basis for the development of common understanding and common action.

The intricate task of getting people to bridge the differences that arise from the singularity of their experience requires a disciplined approach to knowledge. Knowledge is socially powerful only if it is knowledge that can be put to use. Social knowledge, if it is to be useful, must be communicable, valid, and compelling.

In order to be **communicable**, knowledge must be expressed in clear form. And if the knowledge is intended to be used as a spur to action, it must be **valid** in light of the appropriate evidence and **compelling** in the way that it fits the question raised. A personal opinion such as "I think climate change is caused by humans" may influence your friends and even your relatives to think that they are contributing to global warming. But it probably will not make any waves with others. If, however, you can cite evidence that there is more carbon dioxide in the atmosphere today than there has been in the past 650,000 years and that global temperatures are rising as a result, you have a more compelling argument because you relate a judgment to measurements of reality.[1] People who do not even like you but who favor efforts to prevent catastrophes associated with global warming might find such a statement a powerful cue to examine critically the major sources of human-caused carbon dioxide, such as coal. Knowledge built on evidence, and captured in clear transmissible form, makes for power over the environment.

Accumulating knowledge so that past mistakes can be avoided has always intrigued civilized humanity. One can record the sayings of wise people, and that does contribute greatly to cultural enrichment. Yet there is surely room for another kind of cumulative effort: the building up of statements evidenced in a manner that can be double-checked by others. To double-check a statement requires that one know precisely what was claimed and how the claim was tested. This is a major part of the enterprise of science. The steps discussed in Chapter Two, in the section on the scientific method, are the guideposts for accomplishing that kind of knowing.

THE ROLE OF REASONED JUDGMENT AND OPINION

All this vaguely ominous talk about systematic thinking is not meant to cast out reasoned judgment, opinion, and imagination. After all, there is no particular sense in limiting the facilities of the mind in any inquiry.

Reasoned judgment is a staple of human understanding. A reasoned judgment bears a respectable relationship to evidence. Because people inevitably have to act in the absence of complete evidence for decision making, the term *judgment* is important.

Judgment connotes decision making in which all the powers of the mind are activated to make the best use of available knowledge.

Social science does not eliminate the role of judgment from the research process. Indeed, judgment plays a crucial role in how scientific evidence is gathered and evaluated. We can observe that the highest-earning 1 percent of Americans collected more than 23 percent of all income by 2007—more than double their share in 1980. The top 1 percent saw their incomes increase by 256 percent from 1980 to 2007. During that same period, the income of the typical American increased by just 21 percent despite American workers becoming more productive than ever. It is another matter, however, to link this evidence to broad social questions about inequality, poverty, wealth, class, productivity, economic development, and other issues. Logic and good judgment are required to interpret the evidence.[2]

Reasoned judgment is the first part of systematic thought. The proposition that "A full moon on the eve of election day promotes liberal voting" could be correct. However, it does not reflect much reasoned judgment because there is neither evidence for linking the two events nor a logical connection between them. An investigator with time and resources might look into such a proposition, but in a world of scarce time, inadequate resources, and serious problems of social analysis to engage rare talents, such an investigation makes little sense.[3] Although the proposition may be intuitive, even intuition usually bears some relationship to experience and evidence.

Opinion, likewise, plays an inescapable role in scientific analysis because all efforts at inquiry proceed from someone's personal interest. No one asks a question unless there is curiosity about what the conclusion might be. Furthermore, each person's angle of vision on reality is necessarily slightly different from another person's angle. Opinion cannot be eliminated from inquiry but it can be controlled so that it does not fly off into complete fantasy. One practice that assists in reducing the role of opinion is for the researcher to be conscious of his or her values and opinions.

Plato's famous aphorism "know thyself" applies here. Much damage has been done to the cause of good social science by those who pretend **objectivity** to the point at which their research conceals opinions that covertly structure their conclusions. No one is truly objective, certainly not about the nature of society—there are too many personal stakes involved for that.

Ultimately, good science provides its own check on the influence of values in an inquiry. If the method by which the study has been done and the evidence for conclusions are clearly and fully stated, the study can be examined by anyone for the fit of conclusions to evidence. If there is doubt about the validity of what has been done, the study itself can be double-checked, or "replicated," to use the technical term. This feature distinguishes science from personal judgment and protects against personal bias.

No one can double-check everything that goes on, as the mind deals with inner feelings, perceptions of experience, and thought processes. Science brings the steps of inquiry out of the mind and into public view so that they can be shared as part of the process of accumulating knowledge.

THE ROLE OF IMAGINATION, INTUITION, AND CUSTOM

The mind, in its many ways of knowing, is never so clever or so mysterious as in the exercise of **imagination**. If there is any sense in which people can leap over tall obstacles in a single bound, it is in the flight of the mind. But it is one thing to imagine a possible proposition about reality and quite another to start imagining evidence.

Science is really a matter of figuring out relationships between things we can observe. To propose a relationship between things is a creative and imaginative act; however, much systematic preparation may lie in the background. To test a proposition against reality involves a different order of imagination—mainly, the ability to find in the bits and pieces of information elicited from reality the items that are essential to testing the credibility of the idea about a relationship.

It is in the realm of discovery that science becomes a direct partner of imagination. The history of natural science is filled with examples, from the realization that the earth revolves around the sun and not vice versa, to the discovery that matter is made up of tiny atoms. Each discovery was made by bold and imaginative people who were not afraid to challenge a whole structure of customary belief by consulting evidence in the real world. Although these were discoveries on a grand scale, the same sort of effort is involved in stepping outside accepted explanations of human behavior to imagine other possibilities and test them by the intelligent use of evidence. Gender scholars do this when they examine traditional claims about male–female differences. To be truly imaginative is something like trying to escape gravity—the initial move is the hardest. Even though the social sciences have as yet few discoveries to compare with the feats of natural science, the application of science to social relations is a much more recent and vastly more complicated undertaking.[4]

At a fundamental level, scientific inquiry is motivated by curiosity and a desire to find order in what may seem to be chaos. We see an array of confusing events, incidents, and behaviors and have an urge to know why something happened or what event caused another. Social science allows us to satisfy our curiosity and to gain understanding for its own sake. On another level, social science produces knowledge that is communicable and can be used to explain our understanding to others.

Whatever we may come to say about the careful thinking that scientific analysis requires, there is still no way to capture completely the wondrous process of "having an idea." Science is absolutely not a system for frustrating that exercise of intuition and imagination; rather, it is a set of procedures for making such ideas as fruitful and productive as human ingenuity allows. Even the most wonderful idea is only as good as its relationship to some present or potential reality. Science is the art of reality testing, of taking ideas and confronting them with observable evidence drawn from the phenomena to which they relate.

To step back from the general blur of human relationships and envision alternative possibilities demands a level of imagination that is as uncommon as it is necessary. In the usual run of social and political experience, David Hume's observation may be sadly accurate, "[People], once accustomed to obedience, never think of departing from that path in which they and their ancestors trod and to which they are confined by so many urgent and visible motives."[5] Yet it is in the understanding and reform of social and political arrangements that the world requires the very best application of disciplined imagination. In the absence of imaginative efforts to understand the reality of society, we are confined to the beaten path of custom and the inequities that stifle human potential.

We also may be confined to some very unproductive habits of behavior. It used to be the custom in England to hang pickpockets publicly in order to discourage others in the trade. Someone noticed, however, that more pockets were picked at pickpocket hangings than at other public events. The custom survived that bit of social science far longer than it should have.

Custom is not all bad, for it may embody the lessons learned from a long, often unhappy, experience with reality—and it is, in a vague way, scientific. Custom frequently holds communities together in the face of enormous and even violent pressures. Yet the task of any social scientist must be to understand why things are the way they are, as well as how the elements of social life can be reformed to allow for more humane patterns of personal development and expression. The weapons in this struggle for understanding are not only science, with its procedures for disciplining inquiry, but also the intuition that life can be better than it is, that a given pattern of behavior may be other than inevitable, that even the smallest transactions of behavior may contain the keys to larger structures of possibility and potential.

The method of any effort at understanding involves a tension between thought and investigation. There are various ways of linking these two components. The mystic perceives an inner truth and interprets "signs" as validation of the insight. The historian looks for patterns in the past and then suggests their usefulness in interpreting the meanings of events. Thus, the "rise of the middle class" in Europe becomes a major interpretive concept for the historian. Someone who is scientific attempts to be more concrete than the mystic and more precise than the historian with respect to the thoughts by which research is guided, the data regarded as significant in the investigation, and the measures used in testing mental constructions against reality.

In the chapters that follow, we look at each step involved in building scientific understanding. As you will see, the technique requires common sense more than technical knowledge or elaborate preparation.

CONCEPTS INTRODUCED

Science	Valid knowledge	Objectivity
Technology	Compelling knowledge	Imagination
Communicable knowledge	Reasoned judgment	Custom
	Opinion	

QUESTIONS FOR DISCUSSION

1. What are examples of nonscientific modes of understanding? How might these nonscientific modes be used to explain the following:

    -   Why are some people wealthier than others?
    -   Why do political revolutions occur in some places but not in others?
    -   Who will win next year's Super Bowl?

2. How is social scientific knowledge more powerful than other forms of knowledge (such as intuition or custom)? What are its shortcomings and dangers?

3. How might scientific knowledge be useful to someone who is concerned with reforming or changing society?

4. Why is imagination essential to social science?

5. Is the application of imagination more important to social science than to natural science (such as chemistry or biology)?

ENDNOTES

1. See *Climate Change 2007: Synthesis Report Summary for Policymakers* (Valencia, Spain: 2007). Intergovernmental Panel on Climate Change, p. 5.

2. Jacob Hacker and Paul Pierson, *Winner-Take-All Politics* (New York: Simon & Shuster, 2010). "The Rich, the Poor and the Growing Gap Between Them: Rich Are Big Gainers in America's New Prosperity," *Economist* (June 15, 2006). Thomas Piketty and Emmanuel Saez, "The Evolution of Top Income Groups: A Historical and International Perspective," *NBER working paper 11955* (January 2006). These studies showed that the income gap between rich and poor was the largest since 1921 and was growing.

3. Police and bartenders will tell you that the night of a full moon does, in fact, bring out some pretty bizarre behavior; the hypothesis is not completely preposterous.

4. Perhaps one of the earliest attempts to confront social custom with science was the effort in the late nineteenth century by Francis Galton, an English scientist, to test the efficacy of prayer. Observing that prayers were daily offered in churches throughout the land for the long life of royalty, he compared their longevity to that of the gentry and a variety of professionals. He found, after excluding deaths by accident or violence, and including only those who survived their thirtieth year, that the average age of decease for royalty was 64.04 years, the lowest for all his categories. Galton did observe, however, that prayer has many

personal uses aside from the fulfillment of requests. And, who knows, royalty might have died sooner but for such petitions. P. B. Medwar, *Induction and Intuition in Scientific Thought* (Philadelphia: American Philosophical Society, 1969), pp. 2–7.

5.   David Hume, "Of the Origins of Government," In Charles Hendel, ed. *Political Essays* (New York: Liberal Arts Press, 1953), p. 41.

2

The Elements of Science

The Origin and Utility of Concepts

What is a Variable?

Quantification and Measurement: Turning Concepts into Variables

Reliability and Validity of Variables

The Hypothesis

The Scientific Method

The Many Roles of Theory

> [Scientific inquiry] begins as a story about a Possible World—a story which we invent and criticize and modify as we go along, so that it ends by being, as nearly as we can make it, a story about real life.
>
> —P. B. MEDAWAR

To see scientific thought in the context of other kinds of thinking, as we have tried to do, tells us why we should be interested in science. Now it is time to see what science is made of.

The elements of a scientific strategy are, in themselves, simple to understand. They are concepts, variables, hypotheses, measurements, and theories. The way in which these are combined constitutes the scientific method. It is the function of theory to give meaning and motivation to this method by enabling us to interpret what is observed. First, we will try to put each element in place.

THE ORIGIN AND UTILITY OF CONCEPTS

If you had to purge all words and other symbols from your mind and confront the world with a virgin mind, what would you do? Without a body to sustain, you might do nothing. The necessities of survival, however, start closing in, and the first act of the mind might be to sort out the edible objects from the inedible, then the warm from the cold, the friendly from the hostile. From there it is not very far to forming concepts such as food, shelter, and warmth and symbolizing these concepts in the form of words or utterances. Thus, humbly, emerges the instrument called language. The search for truly usable concepts and categories is under way. Languages are huge collections of **concepts**—names for things, feelings, and ideas generated or acquired by people in the course of relating to each other and to their environment.

Some concepts and classifications might not be very helpful. To conceptualize all plants under a single designation would preclude further distinctions between those that are edible, those that heal, and those that poison. Some concepts relate to experience too vaguely: English has but one word for something so varied and complicated as love. Greek allows three concepts: *eros* for romantic love, *agape* for generalized feelings of affection, and *filios* for family love. The inadequacy of English in dealing with the concept of love affects everyone's experience through the tricky ways that the word is used in our culture.

Notice that reality testing is built right into the process of naming things. That back and forth between the stimuli of the environment and the reflections of the mind makes up the kind of thought we will be trying to capture for analysis.

After several thousand years of human history, we still have to face the fact that the process of naming things is difficult. Language emerges essentially by agreement. You and I and the other members of the family (or tribe, state, nation, world) agree, for example, to call things that twinkle in the sky *stars*. Unfortunately, these agreements may not be very precise. In common usage, the term *star* covers a multitude of objects, big and small, hot and cold, solid and gaseous.

To call a thing by a precise name is the beginning of under-standing, because it is the key to the procedure that allows the mind to grasp reality and its many relationships. It makes a great deal of difference whether an illness is conceived of as caused by an evil spirit or by bacteria on a binge. The concept *bacteria* is tied to a system of concepts in which there is a connection to a pow-erful repertoire of treatments, including antibiotics.

To capture meaning in language is a profound and subtle pro-cess, even if it is a little sloppy. For example, the abstract concept *race* expresses differences in the ways that groups are identified. When names are given to categories or properties of race, the pro-blems, power, and difficulty of naming things become evident. Researchers often name people "white" or "nonwhite" (or "An-glo" or "non-Anglo") when using simplistic classifications of race. Such a distinction, although common practice, trivializes differ-ences among a large portion of the world's people. Also, the names themselves can raise complex issues. Think of the various names used in the United States to refer to African Americans (Negro, African American, person of color, black) or Hispanic Americans (Latino, Latina, Hispanic, person of color, Latin American, Mexi-can American, Central American, Puerto Rican, and so forth).

Naming is a process that can give the namer great power. Properties of the concept *race* are not easily named. Names of races, moreover, confer different identities on different people. In your own expression of social scientific thinking, although you are invited to be precise about concepts, you are not invited to be arrogant about the utility of your new knowledge for re-working lives, societies, and civilizations.

The importance of having the right name for a thing can hardly be overestimated. Thomas Hobbes, a seventeenth-century English political theorist, thought the proper naming of things so important to the establishment of political order that he made it a central function of the sovereign. King James understood the mes-sage and ordered an authoritative translation of the Bible as a way of overcoming violent squabbles about the precise meanings of words in the Scriptures.

More germane to the modern scene, George Orwell, in his anti-utopian novel *1984*, gave us a vision of a whole bureaucracy devoted to reconstructing language concepts to enhance the power of a totalitarian society. In recent U.S. political history,

American presidents have attempted to defuse controversy about unpopular wars that they conducted by redefining the concept of military success. These examples are intended to make you aware that by cynically manipulating the meanings of concepts, one can play with the foundations of human understanding and social control.

But it will be a while before you master the scientific method sufficiently to pull off anything very grand. For now, the point is that for scientific purposes, concepts are (1) tentative, (2) based on agreement, and (3) useful only to the degree that they capture or isolate some significant and definable item in reality.

What have concepts got to do with science? If you have spent any time around babies, you might notice that they often try to show off by pointing at things and naming them. It gets a little boring the tenth or fifteenth time through, but babies take justifiable pride in the exercise. Next come sentences. From naming things, from being able to symbolize something rather than simply pointing at it, comes the next step in moving reality around so that it can produce things that are needed. The first sentence Andrew Hoover spoke was to his sister, Erin. Sitting on a little cart, he said, "Erin, push me!" She did.

What you are reading now is an effort to link concepts in order to expand your understanding. People speak sentences by the thousands in an attempt to move reality to some useful response. Most people do not have the good luck that Andrew did on his first try. Often, the concepts are confusing and the connections vague or unlikely, not to mention the problem that the speaker has with the listener's perceptions and motives.

Thought and theory develop through the linking of concepts. Consider, as an example, Pierre Proudhon's famous proposition "Property is theft!" *Property*, as a concept, stands for the notion that a person can claim exclusive ownership of land or other resources. *Theft*, of course, means the act of taking something without justification. By linking these two concepts through the verb *is*, Proudhon meant to equate the institution of private property with the denial of humankind's common ownership of nature's resources. The concept of privately owned property was, he thought, unjustifiable thievery. Although Proudhon's declaration illustrates the linkage of concepts at the lofty philosophical level, the humblest sentence performs the same operation.

Science is a way of checking on the formulation of concepts and of testing the possible linkages between them through references to observable phenomena. The next step is to see how scientists turn concepts into something that can be observed. When concepts are defined as variables, they can be used to form a special kind of sentence, the hypothesis.

WHAT IS A VARIABLE?

A **variable** is a name for something that is thought to influence (or be influenced by) a particular state of being in something else. Heat is one variable in making water boil, and so is pressure. Age has been established as a modestly important variable in voting. However, there are many other more significant variables including socioeconomic standing, parental influence, race, gender, region of residence, and so on.

A variable is, in addition, a special kind of concept that contains within it a notion of degree or differentiation. Temperature is an easily understood example of a variable. It includes the notion of more or less heat—that is, of degree. As the name suggests, variables are things that vary. Interesting questions in social science center on concepts that can be discussed in terms of variation. We are interested in how changes in one phenomenon help to explain variation in another.

Consider, as an example, the relationship between religion and voting. In the first place, religion is a different kind of variable than, say, temperature. Although there may be such a thing as degrees of "religiosity,"[1] we might also discuss variation in the concept *religion* in terms of religious denominations such as Buddhist, Christian, and Muslim. There is substantial variation in the religions with which people identify. For example, exit poll data were used to assess the importance of religion in the 2008 election when Democratic presidential candidate Barack Obama challenged Republican candidate John McCain. Data collected by a consortium of media firms found that fully 78 percent of Jewish voters supported Obama (compared with 21 percent for McCain), whereas 65 percent of white Protestants voted for McCain (compared with 34 percent for Obama). Fifty-four percent of Catholics voted for Obama, while 45 percent voted for McCain. Obama won 75 percent of the votes from those reporting no religious affiliation, while McCain won 67 percent of the vote from Protestants who attended church weekly.[2] Data such as these permit us to say something meaningful about the relationship between the variable *religion* and the variable *voting behavior.*

Although most variables deal with differences of degree, as in temperature, or differences of variety, as in religion, some variables are even simpler. These deal with the most elementary kind of variation: present or absent, there or not there, existent or nonexistent. Take pregnancy, for example. There is no such thing as a little bit of it. Either the condition exists or it does not.

Turning concepts into variables, dull as it may seem, is a very creative process and often raises intriguing questions. Consider, as an illustration, such an ordinary variable as *time.* The early Greeks puzzled a good deal over how to turn this concept into a variable. It seems obvious that time has to be thought of as having a beginning—so philosophers went about trying to figure out when the beginning was. Yet the nagging question always popped up, what happened before that?

Plato and Aristotle both played with the idea that time might not be linear at all, that is, it might not have a beginning, a progression, and presumably an end. It just might be cyclical! This seems crazy to us children of linear time, but they were thinking that universal time might be something like the cycle of the body, a rhythm found everywhere in nature. Historic time, therefore, might best be conceived of as an unfolding structure of events in which one follows the other until the whole pattern is played out and the entire cycle starts over again. Aristotle commented that it just might be that he himself "was living before the Fall of Troy quite as much as after it, since, when the wheel of fortune had turned through another cycle, the Trojan War would be re-enacted and Troy would fall again."[3]

The social science done by introductory students seldom involves such mind-boggling conceptual problems, yet it would not do to pretend that these problems do not exist. The variable *personality,* for example, is reputed to have more than 400 definitions in the professional literature, partly because personality is a compound of a huge range of other variables such as class, status, self-concept, race, socialization, and so forth. The complexity of personality as a variable has driven social scientists to such awkward definitions as "one's acquired, relatively enduring, yet dynamic, unique system of predispositions to psychological and social behavior."[4]

Even when social scientists agree on the description of a variable, that does not mean that the definition possesses the qualities of eternal truth—it just means that some people who have thought about it carefully agree that a given definition seems to help answer some questions. Moreover, researchers often settle on a definition of a variable for reasons of convenience. Identification with political parties in the United States is conventionally measured using responses to survey questions that place voters on a continuum reflecting their identification with the two major political parties. The continuum is represented by this seven-point scale:

← strong Dem — weak Dem — Ind leaning
Dem — Ind — Ind leaning Rep — weak Rep — strong Rep →

Political independents are assumed to be in the center of the political spectrum. Yet the truth of the matter might be that many "independents" think of themselves as radicals who are outside the center. Some might be so nonpartisan or apolitical that they just do not think of themselves in terms of political parties at all. Furthermore, some "leaning" independents are nearly as partisan in their voting as "weak" partisans.[5] Although this definition of the variable might not perfectly reflect the underlying truth of the concept partisanship, it continues to have predictive power. The question has been asked on surveys for decades, so it allows researchers to evaluate trends in partisanship over time. As the difficulties of categorizing independents on this spectrum become apparent, new definitions of partisanship will emerge. Ignoring the problem of specifying how concepts should be turned into variables does not make the problem go away; it just gets you further into the linguistic soup.

The huge stock of concepts in language creates enormous possibilities for linking up variables to explain events. People have muddled around for centuries trying to sort through significant connections. Science is a slightly elevated form of muddling by which these connections are tried out and tested as carefully as possible. In medical science, it took centuries to isolate the many variables affecting disease. Only recently has medical science become so disciplined that it can diagnose many diseases through highly significant blood-chemistry analysis. This development

represents the present stage of a long process of isolating and eliminating a host of unimportant or marginally significant variables.
Increasingly in the West, doctors come up against an ancient
form of medicine developed to a high art in China, and now we
have medical scientists trying to figure out how acupuncture
works. New sets of variables must be considered, new conceptual
bridges built, and the resistance of conventional understanding
overcome.

Unfortunately for social science, we have barely figured out how
to lay the foundation for a structure of theory to explain social behavior. Many new students of social science do not see—especially
when confronted by thick texts in introductory courses—the context
of struggle and accomplishment, tentativeness and probability, behind what has been achieved in social understanding.

Social science currently contains many subdivisions (including
political science, sociology, economics, psychology, and education), all of which are working to define, observe, and link specific
variables within subsystems of behavior. Social scientists are in the
process of chasing a good many possible connections between
variables. The bits of tested knowledge that do emerge await an
integration across the lines of these inquiries. Relatively few have
been attempted, though these efforts are bound to increase in view
of the dramatic need for comprehensive social understanding.

Quantification and Measurement: Turning Concepts into Variables

We said earlier that social scientists turn concepts into variables.
This is done so the concept can be expressed in a form that is
observable and includes some notion of degree or differentiation.
The next question is, how does one pin down that degree or differentiation? The answer involves a two-step process: quantification and measurement.

The idea of quantification means setting up a standard amount
of a thing and putting a label on it. When we do this, we make it
possible to express abstract concepts (such as length) in a manner that
provides a common reference for observation. The origins of some
quantifications are pretty strange. The ancient Greeks, for example,
needed a standard quantity of distance, so they settled on the length
of Hercules's foot. For a long time the foot competed with the cubit,

which was the length of someone else's forearm. The trouble with the cubit was that people could never agree on how long the standard forearm was—some said 17 inches, some said 21 inches. Consequently we do not hear much about cubits anymore.

Isolating standardized units increases the power of description and analysis. When Gabriel Fahrenheit established the idea of a degree of temperature, he made a much more useful description of hot and cold possible. It makes a considerable difference with respect to a puddle of water if the temperature is 32 degrees rather than 33 degrees; the words *cold* and *colder* do not work very well for capturing that vital degree of difference.

Quantification in social science takes two forms: discrete and continuous. **Discrete quantification** relates to counting the presence or absence of a thing. It also relates to counting differences of quality as they are captured in categories. A vote for a candidate is a discrete and specific act that can be counted in a conventional manner. A person's sex is a quality that can be counted as being male, female, or transgender.

Some quantifications, however, have to capture the notion of variation along a continuum. Age is an example of a **continuous quantification**. True, one can count the number of years in a person's age, but the quantification of age is an expression of something that is ongoing. A reader of this book may be 20.72 years old today; in a few weeks, she will be 21 years old. Continuous quantification deals not with discrete items but with dimensions such as age, length, and time. The mark of continuous quantification is that the variable involved may have any value on a scale, whereas in discrete quantification, only whole numbers appear (such as in counting sheep).

Each variable has its own peculiar problems and potentials for quantification. One distinguishing characteristic of a well-developed science is the array of quantifiable variables that are useful to people working in the field. One mark of a smart scientist is the ability to find ways to quantify important variables in a reliable and meaningful way. Economics has come a long way by using money as a unit of analysis (though economists, among others, sometimes confuse money with value). Many powerful economic indicators, such as the gross domestic product or the consumer price index, are based on money.

Unfortunately for the other social sciences, there are not such easily quantifiable units for measuring power or representing psychological stress, alienation, happiness, personal security, or, for that matter, value. Yet inventive scientists have found more or less successful ways of capturing quantifiable pieces of these variables. A text in any of these areas contains dozens of illustrations of how concepts are turned into quantifiable variables, and we will see some of them in the next chapter. The importance of quantification is that when it can be accomplished, there is potential for more precise measurement.

Measurement is not something we choose to do or not do—it is inherent in every analytic discussion. If you doubt this, in the next conversation you have with someone, listen carefully and notice your dependence on terms that imply measurement. A simple political statement such as, "Democrats generally favor a public role in health care," involves several bits of measurement. The verb *favor* implies degrees of difference; the terms *public* and *health care* can have several meanings; and *Democrats* is a classification. The modifier *generally* attempts to qualify the measurement by indicating that it is not a universal characteristic of all Democrats.

If quantities can be established, measurement becomes much easier. The most obvious measurement deals with the problem of how much: how much distance, how much money, and so forth. Some questions of how much are not so easy to measure—public opinion, for example. Using responses to questions as the quantifiable unit of analysis, one crude survey technique provides respondents a "forced choice" and divides opinion into favorable versus unfavorable. Here, opinion is quantified as a discrete, categorical variable: are you for it or against it? Public-opinion polling is often done on this basis. One thing such a simple measurement conceals, of course, is the intensity of the opinion. On many political issues there may be minorities who are passionately on one side and majorities who are lukewarmly on the other side. Some public-opinion polls deal with this by using five categories instead of two:

> strongly for — somewhat for — neither for nor
> against — somewhat against — strongly against

A political system that simply acts on majority sentiment without taking intensity into account can get itself into a lot of trouble—as the United States did over the Iraq War. A large but rather unenthusiastic majority of the public initially supported the war when

President George W. Bush ordered the initial invasion on March 20, 2003. In less than one year, majority support dissipated. Nine years later, as U.S. personnel were withdrawing from Iraq after nearly 4,500 U.S. military fatalities, opinion reversed with large majorities opposing the war and claiming that it was not worth fighting.[6]

A fancier way of measuring intensity of preferences is to measure opinion in terms of degree. Some surveys ask people to evaluate candidates or parties on a "feeling thermometer" scale where 0 is negative, 50 is neutral, and 100 is positive. To help reveal more accurately the state of opinion, we also want to account for how many people are able to rank something on the scale.[7]

Consider the responses to "feeling thermometer" questions asked in 2011 about candidates for the 2012 Republican presidential nomination. As Table 2.1 illustrates, Mitt Romney was rated highest among all respondents, but, early in the contest, other candidates were rated more highly by Republican voters. Table 2.1

T A B L E   2.1   Measuring Feelings about 2012 Republican Presidential Candidates

Candidate	Average Rating, %	People Unable to Rank, %
All respondents' ratings of candidates		
Mitt Romney	50.4	23
Tim Pawlenty	48.4	67
John Huntsman	47.9	84
Ron Paul	46.3	34
Michele Bachmann	45.6	55
Rick Santorum	43.9	63
Newt Gingrich	42.7	17
Republican respondents' ratings of candidates		
Tim Pawlenty	68.1	63
Michele Bachmann	65.8	57
Mitt Romney	63.1	15
Newt Gingrich	61.9	14
Rick Santorum	60.6	60
John Huntsman	58.2	88
Ron Paul	56.5	33

SOURCE: Quinnipiac University poll archived at http://www.quinnipiac.edu/institutes-and-centers/polling-institute/national/release-detail?ReleaseID=1564. Accessed June 15, 2012.

For Example

___

Religion and Religiosity as Variables

Religion is a complex phenomenon. It can mean membership in a group or a personal feeling. People may think of themselves as part of a particular religion because of how they were raised or due to choices they made. One major study measured this by asking people, "What is your religion, if any?" Respondents were free to offer any reply. The result was a variable that measured a personal, subjective sense of religion. The most common response was "Catholic," followed by "Baptist," "no religion," and "Christian." Others offered many different responses that defined their personal religion.

Identification with a particular religion does not necessarily mean that someone is religious. A person may identify as Catholic, but never attend mass nor believe in Church doctrine. Religiosity is a different concept than religion. How do we translate it into a variable? One way is to ask people about behavior and beliefs that are assumed to reflect piety and being religious. One study asked people, "Do you believe that Jesus Christ is the son of God, or do you believe that Jesus Christ is not the son of God?" This might help us measure religiousness of Christians, but not Jews, Sikhs, and other non-Christians. A broader measure asks people how often they attend religious services and how much religion provides them guidance in day-to-day living. Scholars may debate how to best measure religiosity, but their measures allow us to test how religious identification, and religiosity, are associated with human behavior.

SOURCE: American Religious Identification Survey (ARIS) 2008. Barry Kosimin and Ariela Keysar, Principle Investigators. Trinity College, Hartford, CT.

also illustrates that Tim Pawlenty and Michele Bachmann were viewed more warmly than Romney among Republicans who could rank the candidates, but Romney was much better known. Romney won the nomination.

Reliability and Validity of Variables

Quantified measurement of variables, properly conceived and executed, has the potential for specifying differentiation and degree more effectively than fuzzy words in vague sentences. However we decide to measure variables, we hope to find a method of counting that would provide reliable results if it were to be used by other researchers.

As an example, we could decide to measure presidential approval by asking a random sample of respondents if they like or dislike the president, thereby forcing a choice between only two alternatives. We might expect that other researchers could use the same measure the next day with a comparable random sample and produce results similar to ours.

Conversely, we might ask the first four people we see on a bus to "discuss what they think" about the president. We could then rate presidential approval based on our personal impression of their responses. Other researchers using this measure the next day on the same bus might produce wildly different results. The answers might be vague, and the values influencing the interpretation may differ.

Measurement of a variable is said to have **reliability** if it produces the same result when different people use it. The forced choice question would probably produce consistent results, because each researcher using comparable samples simply has to count up the number of "likes" and "dislikes" to find a measure of approval. Open-ended discussions with people on the bus, however, require that the researcher interpret a variety of comments that might or might not reflect approval. The answers are meaningful—in some ways even more meaningful than the forced-choice responses measured in a random sample survey. But they are less likely to get us a reliable answer to the question of presidential popularity.

Theoretical concerns about measures of variables can be subtle. Each measure we use is supposed to do a good job of representing the underlying truth of the abstract concept we claim to be representing with a quantified variable. A measure is said to be valid "if it does what it is intended to do."[8] The closer a quantified measure comes to reflecting the definition of the underlying concept the research is concerned with, the more valid the measure is. One of the difficulties of social science is that there are not always clear ways of directly assessing **validity**. For example, the IQ test is a measure that might be used reliably by many researchers attempting to quantify intelligence. It will always be debatable, however, just how accurately this test measures a concept as rich, varied, and powerful as intelligence. IQ tests might be reliable, but are they entirely valid? Validity could be limited if IQ scores are inflated for people who simply have more experience at taking standardized tests.

Improperly conceived measurement is dangerous precisely because it can be so powerful. A tragic and repugnant example was the use of body counts as a key to "progress" in the U.S. effort in the Vietnam War. Newscasts about the war would usually report the military's figures on how many "enemies" were killed each day. The implication was that the more we killed, the faster we would win the war. There were two things wrong with this quantified measurement.

First, it did not measure what some policy makers alleged that it measured, that is, the amount of success or failure in achieving overall objectives in the war. Because the war was at least as much a political and psychological struggle as a military conflict, the body counts were largely useless as an index of success. They might have told the military something about the condition of the enemy, but reliance on them promoted adverse political and psychological effects in the Vietnamese population and in our own. The Vietnamese began to notice that it was mainly people of their own race and nationality who were being killed by Americans, regardless of whatever else the war was about. Americans thus came to be feared rather than welcomed as allies by many Vietnamese. At the same time, Americans began to see themselves as technological warriors wreaking havoc in a poor country.

A second flaw in the measurement was its implementation. Troops in the field were supposed to count enemy dead and report the number. Several factors, however, intervened, including the confusion (sometimes deliberate) about who was the enemy, the error introduced by having more than one person counting in a particular location, and the chain-of-command pressures for a high body count. Consequently, although the body counts kept going up and led to predictions of success in the war, the actual situation deteriorated.[9]

The very important point is that sloppy or invalid measurement can be worse than no measurement at all. Interpreting the results of measurement requires an understanding of the measurement itself. Measurements are only as good as the instrument used to do the measuring. When deciding on how a variable should be measured, the validity of that measure can be considered in a number of ways. A measure can be said to have **predictive validity** if it does a good job predicting something external to the measure. For example, if the SAT and ACT tests used for college admission actually predicted how well a person would do through their undergraduate years, the tests could be seen as valid measures. By this standard, feeling thermometer scores such as those listed in Table 2.1 could be seen as a valid measure of a candidate's prospects if they do a good job predicting who wins and who loses.

Content validity reflects the extent that a measure includes sufficient content that is appropriately related to the concept being measured. Ideally, if we wanted to measure how much a person participates in politics, we would identify a range of behaviors that are related to the concept of "political participation," including voting, joining interest groups, boycotting products, discussing politics with friends, attending meetings, and so on. Because the domain of political participation is expansive, measuring it simply in terms of whether or not someone votes might not be a content-valid measure.

Construct validity may be the most important way to think about validity. This involves the degree that a measure is logically consistent with the underlying concept you seek to measure. Put simply, construct validity is the extent to which the measurement of some thing measures what it is supposed to measure. In most cases with social science, the validity of a measure is not something that is tested or proven, yet the researcher must always be asking, are we really measuring what we think we are?

THE HYPOTHESIS

Although much of the preceding discussion may seem like a serial review of bits and pieces of scientific thinking, a discussion of hypothesis will bring these matters together.

A **hypothesis** is a sentence of a particularly well-cultivated breed. The purpose of a hypothesis is to organize a study. If the hypothesis is carefully formed, all the steps of the scientific method will follow, as does an outline for the project, a list of resources needed, and a specification of the measures appropriate to the study. The hypothesis provides the structure.

A hypothesis proposes a relationship between two or more variables. For example, political participation *increases* with education. This simple assertion can be seen as a hypothesis. It has a subject (the variable *political participation*), a connective verb (a relationship, *increases*), and an object that is said to cause something (the variable *education*).

To illustrate the point further:

- Obesity *increases* with poverty.
- Union members are *more likely* than nonunion members to vote Democratic.

Or, less obviously (and, for exercise, you can identify the variables and relations):

- Absence makes the heart grow fonder.

- An apple a day keeps the doctor away.

- Early to bed, early to rise, makes people healthy, wealthy, and wise.

It is crucial to realize that a hypothesis is a supposition, as the Oxford English Dictionary points out, "which serves as a starting point for further investigation by which it may be proved or disproved...." A hypothesis stands at the beginning, not the end, of a study, although good studies may suggest new paths of fruitful inquiry and new hypotheses.

So far, most of our examples of hypotheses have been quite simple. But to go from the straightforward to the bizarre, let us cite an experience in teaching scientific thinking. A student came to one of us with the following proposal for research:

> The fragile psycho-pathological type of double helical existence issuing from the precarious relationship of the colonizer and the colonized (which figuratively is similar to the relationship of Siamese twins) and their respective interaction within the colonial situation is psychologically effective, which ramifications lead to psychological mal-adjustments, i.e., neuroses which subsequently define the nature of the political particulars therein.

That was just the beginning of the proposal! In all that confusing language, there are lots of variables and many relationships. Sorting it out, however, yields two hypotheses:

1. Colonialism *is associated with* neurotic behavior by colonizer and colonial.

2. This neurotic behavior *influences* the political structure of colonialism.

These two hypotheses, large as they are, are somewhat manageable. The concept *colonialism* describes a well-established political situation. Saying that the relationship *is associated with* was a retreat from saying *causes*—a precaution taken in view of the limited research resources available to the student. Neurotic behavior is a tricky concept, but it has parentage in the literature of psychoanalytic theory;

there are behaviors that can respectably be labeled neurotic. From there it becomes a matter of showing the links between the kinds of neurotic, self-destructive behavior that occur in colonial situations and the repressive and authoritarian patterns of colonial politics.

Had the student accomplished all that these hypotheses imply by way of evidence gathering, measurement, and evaluation, he would have been in line for a doctorate degree. As long as we both knew that he was just scratching the surface, his paper (bravely titled "Colonialism: A Game for Neurotics") was good enough for undergraduate requirements.

One thing that this example illustrates is that there is often a step prior to hypothesis formation. The step is called **problem reformulation**. In the preceding example, we began with a generalized concern about colonialism and neurosis. The student elaborated that concern into a complex description of the problem. We narrowed it down by specifying variables and relationships into something that could be dealt with, at least in a general way. With a workable reformulation, defining the ways that variables are represented becomes easier.

One art of social science is skillful problem reformulation. Reformulation requires, in addition to some analytic common sense, the ability to see the variables in a situation and the possible relationships between them. A good first step is to break the problem into its component variables and relationships. Writing down lists of hypotheses associated with a problem enables you to select the ones that answer two questions: Which hypotheses are crucial to the solution of the whole problem? For which hypotheses is there information within the range of your resources? Sometimes these questions force some unpleasant choices, but they help prevent arriving at the end of a research effort with nothing substantial on which to hang a conclusion. The preceding example on colonialism and neurosis illustrates the point.

The importance of establishing a hypothesis correctly before starting off on a research task can hardly be overstated. The following rules will help:

1. The variables must be clearly specified and measurable by some technique you know how to use.
2. The relationship between the variables must be precisely stated and measurable.

3.   The hypothesis should be testable, so that evidence of the relationship can be observed, demonstrated, or falsified.

If these rules are not followed, the hypothesis may be unwieldy, ridiculous, or just too hard to research in view of available resources. Precise definitions and thoughtful specification of measurements are, in short, the keys. The struggle to form a hypothesis carefully may not be enjoyable, but the questions raised in the process have to be answered sooner or later.

The hypothesis, then, provides the structure for your entire research effort, whether it involves interviews and surveys, analysis of previously collected data, library research, or all three. It will direct you to relevant information so that you do not waste time and effort. The variables you have selected can be researched through library search engines, Internet resources such as Google Scholar, book indexes, periodical guides, online services, and other computer database searches. The relationships proposed between the variables suggest the measurement tools and standards for evaluation that you will need to use. The results of the hypothesis test are the substance of your conclusions.

Once relationships between variables have been established through hypothesis formation and testing, these relationships can be expressed as **generalizations**. Generalizations based on tested relationships are the object of science. A generalization is a hypothesis affirmed by testing. As generalizations in a field of study accumulate, they form the raw stuff of theories. But this gets us ahead of the story. For now, we need to see how the scientific method sets the procedure for research into a logical sequence.

THE SCIENTIFIC METHOD

The technique known as the **scientific method** is quite commonsensical. The model inquiry proceeds by steps that include the following:

1.   Identify the variables to be studied.

2.   Form a hypothesis about the relation of one variable to another or to a situation.

3.   Perform a reality test whereby changes in the variables are measured to see if the hypothesized relationship is evidenced.

4. Compare the measured relationship between the variables with the original hypothesis and develop generalizations about the findings.

5. Provide suggestions about the theoretical significance of the findings, factors involved in the test that may have distorted the results, and other hypotheses that the inquiry brings to mind.

Although we have sketched here the bare bones of the scientific method, the actual procedure of research does not always start directly with hypothesis formation. As a preliminary to stating hypotheses, social scientists often examine the data collected in a subject area to see if there are connections between the variables. The relationships brought to light by various statistical processes frequently suggest the hypothesis it would be fruitful to explore. Occasionally, simply getting involved with a set of data triggers an interesting thought, a chance insight, or a new idea. Because a large quantity of data has been generated over the past few decades, researchers can often avoid having to begin at the beginning with every inquiry. The analysis of existing data can be extremely helpful in identifying new data needed to test a crucial relationship.

This is only an outline of the scientific method. In the hands of a skilled analyst, other elements are introduced, such alternative ways to measure results, detailed conceptual analysis of the variable description, relationships between one's own study and others, assessments of the validity of the measuring instruments, the use of experimental and control groups, and, equally important, careful conjecture that goes beyond what is established in the test itself. These embellishments on the methodology, however, relate more to the tools used to carry out the method than to the method itself.

The point is that the scientific method seeks to test thoughts against observable evidence in a disciplined manner, with each step in the process made explicit.

Consider the differences between two kinds of studies: (1) an empirical scientific study in which the author states his or her ideas about concepts, forms hypotheses about how the concepts are related, lays out a testing procedure, carefully translates concepts into variables that are validly measured, produces a specific result, and relates this to the hypotheses; and (2) a nonscientific study in which the author expresses ideas, develops a general thesis, examines relevant examples, and states the conclusions.

Notice that the tension between thought and investigation is present in both studies. But one important difference is the feasibility of checking the soundness of the conclusions in the first example, as opposed to the second, by repeating the study. Social scientists use the word **replication** to indicate the ability to repeat a study as a way of checking if it is solid. Replication constitutes someone else redoing an existing study in order to find errors that might have crept in through the procedures and evaluative judgments contained in the original study. Good science can be replicated by others.

A second difficulty with a nonscientific study lies in the problem of relating one study to another. One person's idea may be interesting, but if stated without a systematic method to test it, the idea might be difficult to defend.

A good scientific study presents all the information needed to see what took place. For example, if standard variable definitions are used, a study of voters' assessments of candidates can be added to studies of how voters view issues, parties, or whatever. As scientists try to build cumulative bodies of knowledge, different studies of the same variables using different measures can be compared to see if measurement techniques create alternative results. The point, once again, is that science regulates and specifies the relationship between thought and investigation in such a way that others may know exactly what has been done.

THE MANY ROLES OF THEORY

Science rests its claim to authority upon its firm basis in observable evidence about something called "reality." We have occasionally described science as, simply, reality testing. Because everyone thinks he or she knows what reality is, science acquires a fundamental appeal. Yet the necessary partner of realism in science is that wholly imaginary phenomenon, **theory**. Without the many roles that theory plays, there would be no science (and, some would argue, there would be no understandable "reality," either).

Just as language arises out of the experience of coming to grips with human needs, so too does theory arise from tasks that people face. The hardest task is to explain what is really going on out there. Volumes have been written about what theory is and is not. For our purposes, a theory is a set of related propositions that suggest why events occur in the manner that they do.

The propositions that make up theories are of the same form as hypotheses: they consist of concepts and the linkages or relationships between them. Theories are built up as hypotheses are tested and new relationships emerge.

Theory abounds in the most ordinary transactions of life. There are theories of everything from the payoff of slot machines to the inner meaning of Dilbert cartoons. The grandest theories of all are religious and philosophical, embracing huge orders of questions about the origin of the physical universe, the history of the species, the purposes of life, and the norms of behavior that lead to virtue and, possibly, happiness. To the faithful, such theories are made true by a belief in supernatural phenomena. These kinds of theories are presented as if they were embedded in the larger cosmos of our existence, awaiting our arrival at understanding.

Social science, by contrast, generally operates from a different perspective on theory. The most conventional posture of a social scientist is one of pragmatism: a theory is only as good as its present and potential uses in generating hypotheses and explaining observations. The point of any science is to develop a set of theories to explain the events within their range of observation.

It is tempting, but misleading, to conceive of theory as something rock-like and immobile behind the whiz and blur of daily experience. Rather, theory is a sometimes ingenious creation of human beings in their quest for understanding. People create theories in proportion to needs, and the theories they create can be either functional or dysfunctional to those needs. A theory could contain a complete system of categories and generalizations but still be useless. If, for example, one were to categorize the world in terms of tall things and short things and characterize all the relationships between them, a theory would have been born, but it would be one of dubious utility—not false, but useless.

Social science theory is often derived from fundamental assumptions about human behavior. Rational actor theories suggest that individuals, organizations, and nation-states are motivated by a desire to maximize their material interests. Based on this type of theory, we might hypothesize that voters select candidates that further their own economic interest. Alternatively, psychological theories assume that voting actions are determined by people's long-term feelings of attachment for political parties. Voters are thought to be socialized, via the family, to be loyal to a particular party. From this theory, we might hypothesize that voters act like their parents, or that they select candidates of the same party year after year. The origins of wars have been explained by rational actor theories and psychological theories, as well as by Marxian theories and other forms of social theory.

We have been discussing what theory is and is not. The next question is, what does it do? The answer is, many things. We list four particular uses of theory in social scientific thinking:

1. Theory provides patterns for the interpretation of data.
2. Theory supplies frameworks within which concepts and variables acquire substantive significance.
3. Theory links one study with another.
4. Theory allows us to interpret the larger meaning of our findings for ourselves and others.

The four uses of theory are illustrated in the text that follows by looking at the question of voter participation. The rate of voter participation is an important indicator of democracy. It is reasonable to expect that different types of election rules will affect the number of people who think it is worth their time and effort to vote. We will show how theory influences the way we look at questions of political participation under contrasting sets of election rules. The patterns observed in the data, the links established between studies, the substantive significance of the findings, and their larger meaning are all shaped by the theories the researcher uses.

In this illustration, we focus on how election rules translate people's votes into seats for parties in a legislature. In the United States, nearly all elections are for single-member districts. These rules award a single seat to the candidate who wins the most votes in each district. Where the rules allow a wider variety of parties to win seats (as in proportional representation [PR] systems), presumably more people will vote.[10] In PR systems, each party wins a proportion of the total number of seats based on its percentage of the vote. Thus, if 10 legislative seats are to be allocated in an election, most of the seats would likely go to candidates from large parties, but smaller parties can elect candidates to one or two seats by winning 10 or 20 percent of the vote.

Some theorize that winner-take-all rules in single-member districts might reduce participation. In the United States, the rules mean that nearly all seats are won by candidates from the Democratic and Republican parties. The hypothesis would be that citizens who are not oriented toward candidates from the major parties might be discouraged from voting.[11] Because a large slice of the electorate see themselves as "independents," this becomes an important factor in assessing the effectiveness of U.S. democracy.

Consider the data presented in Table 2.2. The table shows the average level of turnout for elections held in various countries under three types of election rules. Winner-take-all rules award seats only to candidates that finish first in a single district. Proportional systems typically allow voters to select a party's slate of candidates, then allocate multiple seats roughly proportionate to each party's vote share. Some nations elect part of their legislature with winner-take-all rules and the rest with proportional rules. These nations have mixed systems.

What message do these data provide? Looking at the top row of data in Table 2.2, we find that election rules might affect participation in national elections. Countries that use PR averaged 72.1 percent turnout, compared with a 62.7 percent turnout rate for the nations that use winner-take-all rules. These data are averages based on elections in different countries. The data suggest,

T A B L E   2.2   Turnout at National Elections, 2002–2012

	Type of Election Rules for National Legislature		
	Winner-take-all[a]	Proportional[b]	Mixed[c]
Average turnout, %	62.7	72.1	73.4
Standard deviation, %	2.9	10.4	6.6
Number of nations	4	12	3
Number of elections	10	34	9

[a]Canada, Great Britain, France, United States
[b]Denmark, Finland, Greece, Iceland, Ireland, Israel, Netherlands, Norway, Portugal, Spain, Sweden, Switzerland
[c]Germany, Japan, New Zealand
NOTE: Average turnout for national elections held in 19 advanced industrialized democracies where voting is largely noncompulsory.

SOURCE: Authors' calculations from data posted at the Institute for Democracy and Electoral Assistance website, http://www.idea.int/. Accessed June 28, 2012.

but do not prove conclusively, that proportional representation influences more citizens to vote. Rival explanations and intervening variables, such as cultural differences, however, might explain these patterns as well.[12]

Where does the theory enter in? What theories fit this pattern of data? One theory is that people are more likely to act—in this case, to vote—when they think their action will have tangible consequences. In other words, they are more likely to vote if they think their most preferred party might win or if they think their vote might make a difference in a close election. Thus, PR systems might attract followers of smaller parties to vote because of the greater likelihood that their vote could have the effect of electing a representative. Because PR allows more parties in a legislature, the data in Table 2.2 seem to support the theory that PR mobilizes a wider range of citizens because their vote is more likely to have a tangible result.

Another theory proposes that people vote out of a sense of civic duty. Under this theory, they vote regardless of perceptions about their preferred party's chances of winning seats.[13] Because we have no data about how the public's sense of civic duty varies across these nations, the fact that our data are consistent with one theory does not mean that we can reject the rival theory.

Being aware of different theories allows social scientists to link their studies with previous research. It also provides a means to generate additional tests that might allow us to reject rival theories that offer alternative explanations for patterns seen in the data. If we found, for example, that there were no differences in perceived civic duty among the places reflected in the data in Table 2.2, a stronger case could be made that PR motivates more people to vote than do winner-take-all elections.

PR might cause the perceived benefits of voting (greater chances of representation) to outweigh the costs. It might be that nonvoters in the United States are those who feel politically marginalized by electoral institutions that prevent their preferred candidates from winning office. Through these links in reasoning, social scientists can accumulate knowledge of relationships between different theoretical constructs. So far we have seen two uses of theory in relation to the example in Table 2.2: the patterns the theory provides and the ways the theory links one study to another.

The third use of theory is now apparent. We need to assess the substantive significance of what is observed here.[14] That is, we need to ask if the observations have implications that are interesting or important. This result could be important for testing the usefulness of rational action theories in explaining political behavior. In this case, we might infer that a switch to PR rules could boost turnout substantially in a nation using winner-take-all elections.[15]

It would seem that giving people more choices in elections might lead to greater citizen participation. This raises a host of interesting substantive questions: How would the participation of these voters change a political system? What new parties might succeed? How would institutions such as Congress function with several parties?

The larger meaning of these findings for theories relating political institutions to human behavior lies beyond these specific substantive questions. Participation in a representative democracy is not just a matter of having the formal right to vote. People are also sensitive to the results of the process and to the constraints that institutions create. Clearly, other factors are involved, but it would seem that election systems that lead to the representation of more social groups also encourage more people to vote. Proportional rules that produce representation for a wider variety of people are also likely to have broader effects on citizens' attitudes about politics and government generally.[16]

In discussing theory, we presented an illustration of its uses in social scientific research. Most researchers are intent on proving their theory to be "right." Karl Popper, an influential analyst of the social sciences, however, shows us that the best use of science is often to refute theories rather than to "prove" them:

> Of nearly every theory it may be said that it agrees with
> many facts: this is one of the reasons why a theory can be
> said to be corroborated only if we are unable to find refuting
> facts, rather than if we are able to find supporting facts.[17]

In other words, data may be more impressive as evidence for the theories they refute than for the theories they support.

What we have not captured in this discussion of theory is the subtlety and creativity with which people think about what they are observing. Theory illuminates observations. Yet, like a beam of light playing on an object, every theory leaves shadows that challenge our imaginations.

On the one hand, we can only say that without theory, social science would be an incoherent and meaningless pile of observations, data, and statistics. On the other hand, not all social science can be tied to rigorous and specific theoretical formulations. It is absolutely clear, however, that complex social problems need all the well-informed study we can develop. The organization and evaluation of that knowledge in theoretical form is almost as important as gathering it in the first place. History is littered with the wreckage of poorly conceived social theories—sometimes with tragic results—though the power of theoretical imagination has been responsible for some of civilization's greatest advances.

We now have in hand the basic tools of scientific thinking. But tools alone do not get the job done. We need a plan or, as described in the next chapter, a strategy for putting those tools to work to produce some knowledge.

CONCEPTS INTRODUCED

Concepts	Reliability	Problem
Variable	Validity	reformulation
Discrete	Predictive validity	Generalizations
quantification	Content validity	Scientific method
Continuous	Construct validity	Replication
quantification	Hypothesis	Theory
Measurement		

QUESTIONS FOR DISCUSSION

1. Consider the concept *unemployment*.

    ▪ How can it be given a definition so that it can be measured as a variable?

    ▪ How many definitions of unemployment can you think of?

    ▪ How do these definitions differ?

2. Evaluate different measures of unemployment in terms of reliability and validity.

    ▪ In terms of reliability, if other researchers used your measures (variables), would they produce similar results?

    ▪ In terms of validity, do the measures do a good job of representing the concept *unemployment*?

3. Consider the data about religion and voting in the 2008 election. Develop a table that expresses the relationship between the two variables. Can you form hypotheses about how (or why) religion is associated with voting?

4. One of the more complex questions that social scientists deal with is, why do people rebel against their governments? Consider three examples of major revolutions (seventeenth-century England, eighteenth-century France, early twentieth-century Russia). Based on these examples, can you form some hypotheses about why revolutions occur? When forming your hypotheses, consider the following:

    ■ What variables are associated with the occurrence of revolutions?

    ■ How do you define concepts such as *revolution?*

    ■ Is your definition something that other researchers could apply reliably to other nations in which revolutions have or have not occurred?

    ■ How are the variables in your hypotheses linked together?

    ■ How would you test the hypotheses?

    ■ Would another person reach the same conclusions as you if he or she used your measures and the tests you suggest?

ENDNOTES

1. Various attempts have been made to measure degrees of individual "religiosity" in terms of attitudinal and behavioral traits such as regularity of church attendance. For an example, see Lyman A. Kellstedt and Mark A. Noll, "Religion, Voting for President and Party Identification, 1948–1984," in *Religion and American Politics: From the Colonial Period to the 1980s*, ed. Mark A. Noll (Oxford, England: Oxford University Press, 1990), p. 347.

2. CNN.com Election 2008 Results. U.S. President Exit Poll. At www.cnn.com/ELECTION/2008/results/polls.main. Accessed June 30, 2012.

3. Stephen Toulmin and June Goodfield, *The Discovery of Time* (New York: Harper & Row, 1965), p. 46.

4. Gordon DiRenzo, *Personality and Politics* (Garden City, N.Y.: Anchor Books, 1974), p. 16.

5. Russell J. Dalton, *The Apartisan American* (Los Angeles: Sage, 2013). The author notes that the American electorate is becoming less partisan overall, but that educated "apartisans" often match their levels of engagement with politics with those of partisans.

6. A CNN poll in late 2011 found just 29 percent saying they favored the war, with 68 percent opposed. A CBS poll taken in late 2011 found just 24 percent saying the war was worth fighting. In April 2003, on the other hand, 75 percent replied that the war was worth fighting. Results archived at www.pollingreport.com/iraq.htm. Accessed June 15, 2012.

7. Problems with nonattitudes are discussed in Herbert Asher, *Polling and the Public: What Every Citizen Should Know*, 7th ed. (Washington, D.C.: Congressional Quarterly Press, 2007), chapter 2.

8. Edward G. Carmines and Richard Zeller, *Reliability and Validity Assessment*. Sage University Paper Series on Quantitative Applications in the Social Sciences, no. 17 (Beverly Hills, Calif.: Sage Publications, 1979).

9. During the Iraq War, the allied military command avoided these problems by not announcing estimates of Iraqi casualties.

10. See, for example, G. Bingham Powell, "American Voter Turnout in Comparative Perspective," *American Political Science Review* 80, no. 1 (1986), p. 1743.

11. One study attempted to hold cultural differences constant by comparing turnout in U.S. local elections that used winner-take-all with those using "semi-proportional" elections. It found that "semi-PR" systems increased turnout by about 5 percent. See Shaun Bowler, David Brockington, and Todd Donovan, "Election Systems and Voter Turnout: Experiments in the United States," *Journal of Politics*, 63, no. 3 (2001), pp. 902–915.

12. Douglas Amy, *Real Choices, New Voices* (Cambridge, UK: Cambridge University Press, 1993), pp. 140–153; Arend Lijphart, "Unequal Participation: Democracy's Unresolved Dilemma," *American Political Science Review* 91, no. 1 (1997), pp. 1–14.

13. For a discussion of these rival theories, see Donald Green and Ian Shapiro, *Pathologies of Rational Choice Theory* (New Haven, Conn.: Yale University Press, 1994). Cf. Kristen Monroe, *The Heart of Altruism: Perceptions of a Common Humanity* (Princeton, N.J.: Princeton University Press, 1996).

14. This should not be confused with statistical significance (see Chapter Five), which tells whether the difference between winner-take-all and PR elections may have occurred by chance. Substantive significance relates to theory rather than to statistical probability.

15. Comparative studies that account for additional variables suggest that the independent effect of PR on turnout varies between 3 and 7 percent. See Andre Blais and Agnieszka Dobrzynska, "Turnout in Electoral Democracies," *European Journal of Political Research* 18 (1998), pp. 167–181; Andres Lander and Henry Milner, "Do Voters Turn Out More Under Proportional Than Majoritarian Systems?," *Electoral Studies*, 18 (1999), pp. 235–250.

16. C. Anderson and C. Guilloty, "Political Institutions and Satisfaction with Democracy: A Cross-National Analysis of Consensus and Majoritarian System," *American Political Science Review* 91, no. 1 (1997), pp. 68–81.

17. In *Popper Selections*, ed. David Miller (Princeton, N.J.: Princeton University Press, 1985), p. 437.

3

Strategies

> A fact is like a sock which doesn't stand up
> when it is empty. In order that a fact may stand
> up, one has to put into it the reason and the
> feeling which have caused it to exist.
>
> —LUIGI PIRANDELLO

Observant readers will notice that two words, usually thought to be integral to the scientific method, rarely appear in this book. They are *fact* and *truth*. What both words have in common is an air of absolutism that misleads those who become involved in the scientific approach to learning. According to its word root, "fact" means "a thing done." That things do get done is not disputed, but the trouble is that "things done" are perceived not by some neutral omnipotent observer but by people.

People have limited powers of observation and structures of instinct and interest that influence how they see the world. *Science is a process for making these observations as explicit and open to examination as possible.* But the results of scientific procedure must always be taken as just that—an *attempt* to control a process that our very humanity makes difficult, if not impossible, to control totally.

For working purposes, social scientists generally regard a **fact** as "a particular ordering of reality in terms of a theoretical interest."[1] Anything identified as a fact is tied to the particular interests that the observer brings to the study of the phenomenon. Further than that we cannot usefully go, for a philosophical forest looms in which subtle questions are raised about whether a tree that falls unobserved has really fallen because we cannot know that it did.

The term **truth** is red meat for philosophers, and they are welcome to it. Science prefers to operate in the less lofty region of **falsifiable statements** that can be checked by someone else. Every good scientific proposition or generalization is stated in such a way that subsequent observations may provide either supporting evidence or evidence that raises questions about the accuracy of the proposition. By making the degree of verification a permanent consideration in science, a good many rash conclusions can be avoided.

The response to this noncommittal attitude toward fact and truth might be, what, then, are we to believe in? If you want something absolute to believe in, it must be found outside of science. Science is a working procedure for answering questions through the refinement of experience. Scientists may develop theories of awe-inspiring power, but the way such theories meet our very human needs for belief is a personal matter separate from the meaning of science for inquiry. To "believe in science" means no more or less than to be committed to judgments based on observations that can be replicated, rather than on some other kind of evidence or mental process.

You are now familiar with basic elements of science, including variables, measurements, and hypotheses. In this chapter we concentrate on how to shape ideas about the world into a form that allows for reality testing. Then the process of reality testing is broken down into its parts. Finally, we see what evaluative steps need to be taken in order to understand the results of research.

The following remarks are designed as a step-by-step guide to scientific analysis. It must be realized, however, that we are trying to capture only the most significant aspects of scientific procedure, not the finer points or the intricacies that a sophisticated researcher would want to introduce. Chapter Four, "Refinements," adds some ideas for increasing the power of your research strategies to each element.

Please bear in mind that all we are doing here is regulating what is natural to human thought: a tension between thought and reality testing. So this chapter is organized into three sections: Thinking Over the Problem, Reality Testing, and Understanding the Results.

THINKING OVER THE PROBLEM

The biggest challenge in doing research occurs at the very beginning. Once you have met that challenge, other steps fall into place. This is the problem of limiting the topic, or, more positively, of selecting an approach to the topic that will most efficiently get at the thing you want to understand. Most students have had the experience of writing a long, rambling, poorly focused paper. As the need for conclusions looms with the final pages, there occasionally arises the awful feeling that no firm conclusion can be reached based on the evidence presented. The reason for such an inglorious end usually can be found in the beginning.

Focus

Because most of us are not trained to think in terms of formulating our ideas into hypotheses and testing them, it is best to start writing things down in the way they occur to the mind: as a sequence of ideas, thoughts, and notions. Ask yourself, why am I interested in this? What is it that I am really after? See what happens. You might start with a broad topic:

> This country is in big trouble. Most people do not think
> that politics matters these days—they do not want to have
> anything to do with it. Politics is such a joke.

Big subjects, but there is a theme here about whether modern democracy works.

At this stage it is a good idea to try to capture these thoughts in a paragraph or two. Get it on paper! Some general reading is a good idea. It helps to map out the areas of investigation. Too much reading may be a bad idea. Do not try to get into your actual research until you have thought through the larger frame of the problem.

Suppose you wind up with two paragraphs like this:

> Something has changed in America. In the old days, it seemed like more people believed that they could make a difference. Maybe they thought that government could make society better, or maybe they just had more free time.
>
> Today, most of the people I talk to do not care about politics and they think elected officials care about special interests, not regular people. Who has the time to get involved with politics? Besides, unless you have money to contribute, they will not listen to you.

These paragraphs actually contain a number of concepts and variables, a network of relationships, and a whole series of hypotheses. But at least there is some indication of the possibilities for a more focused study.

At this point, two levels of study could be mounted: descriptive and relational. A **descriptive study** collects information about a situation. One might describe an institution, event, behavior, or some combination of these. Good description is the beginning of science. Leonardo da Vinci's masterful notes and drawings of human anatomy enabled generations of medical scientists to advance their understanding of the human body. Some specialized descriptive studies analyze information about a single variable, for example, what do people think of same sex marriage? How has opinion changed over time? How much change is going on? Which people become more accepting of it? These studies are valuable sources for higher forms of analysis.

Relational analysis examines connections between things. The basic form consists of probing the links between one variable and another: the relation between trust and being involved with politics, for example, or the relationship between age and having a sense that politics matters. A series of relational studies can form the basis for causal analysis, that special type of relational study in which the most powerful of connections between variables is isolated.

The initial thoughts on the topic given in the preceding paragraphs seem to imply a series of relations. If you are impatient to get to the root of the situation, a relational analysis of some aspect of the general problem of participation and trust might be the next step.

Hypothesis Formation

With the topic narrowed somewhat, hypothesis formation becomes easier. The question is twofold: What are the essential variables? What are the relations between them? One intriguing element of our sample problem involves two variables: *political participation* and *the sense that elected officials care about regular people*. The paragraphs that were written suggest a link between the two different variables. What is the nature of the link? What word expresses that relationship? If we leave aside causal analysis, the suggested relationship is a simple one: People are more likely to participate in politics if they think politicians care about them, rather than special interests. We put aside here the definition of what is "special" and who is "regular."

Even with all these words, we still boil things down to two variables and one relationship: participation *is associated with* political efficacy, that is, with a person's sense that he or she can have influence in politics. Most studies, of course, contain several hypotheses, possibly interconnected as elements of one large thesis. But for purposes of illustration, we will stay with something less demanding.

Operationalizing Concepts

To operationalize a concept means to put it in a form that permits some kind of measurement of variation. In Chapter Two we discussed turning concepts into usable variables; this process is called **operationalization**. Translating a concept into something that allows the observation of variation is a tricky process. If it is done properly, two conditions will be met: (1) the operational version will fit the meaning of the original concept as closely as possible (validity) and (2) the measurement(s) of variation can be replicated by others (reliability).

For Example

Hypothesis Formation for Election Results

Hypotheses are statements that can emerge from simple questions. They are often stated as relationships. An idea might cause us to ask, is x related to y? The idea that led to the question may have had some causal mechanism to it. In this case, the idea is that there is something about x that causes y to happen.

Consider an example from the study of elections. People observed that when the economy did badly (x), incumbents received less support (y). A simple hypothesis then is that incumbents lose support if the economy is poor. We could begin to test this by looking at economic trends and seeing how they correspond with trends in votes for incumbents. Or, at election time we could ask voters how they thought the economy was doing and also ask who they voted for.

Interesting hypotheses often breed additional questions and even more hypotheses. They contain kernels of ideas about what causes what. In this case, what is it about the economy that causes voters to punish incumbents by not reelecting them? Does a voter oppose a candidate because the voter's own personal financial situation became worse or because he or she heard bad news about high unemployment in society? Do voters treat all congressional incumbents the same, or do they reserve extra wrath for candidates from the president's political party?

How does one operationalize whether people are engaged in political activity? Well, how about asking people some simple questions about political participation:

- Did you go to any political meetings, rallies, or speeches?

- Did you do any work for a political party or candidate?

- Have you ever written to a newspaper or a blog about a public matter?

Once the answers are given, it then becomes a matter of identifying patterns in the responses to individual questions or of evaluating how responses to the set of questions hold together. We can look at the responses and see if any themes or trends emerge. We can also look at how many people vote in elections and compare that to trends in attitudes about political efficacy. However we approach it, responses should give us clues about how many people are politically active and whether levels of observed activity match up with levels of observed attitudes.

Trends identified in responses to these questions about political participation can also help us assess our research question. If these questions have been asked over a long period of time, we can see if people are more or less engaged with politics today. The variable *political efficacy* is often measured with responses to this question:

Do you agree or disagree with this statement: Public officials do not care much about what people like me think.

A person's sense of who the government is responsive to has also been measured with responses to this question:

Would you say the government is pretty much run by a few big interests looking out for themselves or is it run for the benefit of the people?

Looking back at the preceding paragraphs, we see that the main hypothesis is about how low levels of efficacy might make people less likely to be engaged with politics today. Normative theories of democracy suggest that a healthy polity needs some minimal level of public participation in the political process.

At this point, we will observe the research strategy actually used in studies by Robert Putnam, a Harvard political scientist. A condensed version of one of Putnam's articles, "Tuning In, Tuning Out: The Strange Disappearance of Social Capital in America," is reprinted as Appendix A in this book.[2]

Putnam offers us another hypothesis. He proposes that low levels of political participation are due, in part, to a decline in membership in voluntary associations. Putnam draws from the works of Alexis de Tocqueville—an early observer of American society—and contemporary sociologist James Coleman to develop his theory and hypotheses.[3] He argues that people are less engaged with politics today than they were in the 1950s because they lack trust in others, trust they learn from working with others in voluntary groups.

Membership in voluntary social groups is expected to somehow transform people, making them more politically engaged. This builds the "civic capacity" that is essential for democracy.[4] The theory goes that Americans from older generations are more active in certain groups that build social trust and social connections. Today, people may be less likely to know their neighbors and less likely to interact with friends.[5] Such connections allow them to see the usefulness of "cooperation for mutual benefit." To oversimplify the argument, a decline in social activity has caused a decline in trust and political activity. If we do not join groups such as the PTA or bowling leagues, for example, we do not learn to trust each other. We thus fail to learn how any collective effort, such as politics, makes any difference. Putnam and others refer to the sum of the social connections, norms, and social trust that we get from group activity as **social capital**.[6] Coleman defines *social capital* as the social connections between individuals that "facilitate action."[7]

Read Putnam's article in Appendix A; it will enhance your understanding as we explore how his research was done. The article is an example of a carefully presented summary of a larger research project. The author begins by discussing the theoretical background of the work, the steps taken in generating and testing hypotheses, and the larger meaning of his results. This is a design to follow—even for a brief research paper.

In operationalizing the variable *political participation*, Putnam examined answers to several questions, including those listed above. He is also interested in how the decline in political participation is associated with trust and with social capital. Social capital, like many concepts in the social sciences, does not provide us an immediately obvious means for operationalization—it is not something we can see or count directly. It is a big concept, and Putnam's theory offers us guidance about what to look for. He suggests that social capital is produced by membership in social groups. This means that one indirect measure of social capital can be answers to simple questions about the social groups a person might join.

Putnam operationalized social capital as social group memberships. He uses responses to survey questions as an instrument to measure group membership. His theory leads him to use membership in the following groups as indicators of social capital:

- Church-related groups
- Sports groups (soccer teams, softball leagues, bowling leagues)
- Arts or literary societies (theater groups, choirs)
- Labor unions
- Fraternal organizations (Lions, Elks, Masons, Jaycees)
- Service clubs
- Civic organizations (Boy Scouts, Red Cross, PTA)

Table 3.1 illustrates how frequently people mentioned being members of some of these groups. Although Putnam is concerned primarily with trends in the United States, these descriptive data show that Americans join social groups at rates that match or exceed those in many other democratic nations. Now, having operationalized the key variable *social capital* in terms of group membership, the stage is set for organizing the whole inquiry and testing his hypothesis. Read how he does this in Appendix A.

T A B L E 3.1   Voluntary Group Membership in 21 Nations

Nation	Religious Group/Club (%)	Sports Group/ Club (%)	Other Voluntary Group (%)
Australia	17	36	23
Austria	8	14	7
Canada	33	35	28
Chile	20	14	7
Czech Republic	4	11	6
Denmark	14	41	26
Finland	7	23	16
France	7	34	26
Germany	15	29	9
Great Britain	17	22	12
Hungary	9	5	3
Israel	11	17	13
Japan	3	13	3
Latvia	9	13	6
Netherlands	15	43	20
New Zealand	17	39	25
Norway	10	28	20
South Korea	12	13	18
Spain	9	15	9
Sweden	7	28	9
United States	40	23	21

NOTE: Group membership is assumed to be one repletion of social capital. Cell entries are percentages of respondents claiming to be a participating member of at least one group in the category.

SOURCE: Authors' analysis of raw data files for the 2004 Citizenship Survey conducted by the International Social Survey Program. Data at www.issp.org.

REALITY TESTING

Organizing the Bibliography

With a hypothesis in mind, it is a good idea to do some additional reading before actually beginning research. This will help you check your formulation of hypotheses and operationalization of variables against other efforts. Use a library database or the Internet to do a search on variables in the hypothesis. Articles, books, and websites are all valuable sources for information and background. Often a single journal article on the topic will contain footnotes and a bibliography that can guide you to most of the significant literature on the subject. A more sophisticated researcher would take this step first—it can save a lot of time in the thinking-it-over stage. Beginning students, however, often come to problems of social analysis "fresh."

Doing Research

Many students might not think of mounting the kind of research enterprise suggested. The survey data we present here are publicly available via the Internet for analysis if you wish to pursue this further.[8] The following examples are for instructional purposes, however, and should be sufficient to show how social science research works so that your own project can be formulated with the clearest possible strategy.

Robert Putnam and others working in this area tested their hypotheses by reanalyzing surveys that had already been done. A lot of social science is carried out in this way. As researchers look at "old" data with a different perspective and a new hypothesis, fresh insights are revealed. In doing your own research, check with faculty members and the library to see if there might be data that you could use to test your hypotheses before you set out to collect your own data.

In this case, scholars often look at data in the General Social Survey (GSS) and the American National Election Study (ANES)—major academic surveys of American attitudes, opinions, and behavior—to examine how trends in social group memberships relate to trends in trust and political participation. This is not the only data source Putnam uses. He draws from other surveys and from records that groups keep about their membership.

Based on his theory, Putnam decided in advance that some types of group memberships are more important than others in building trust and political engagement. Religious groups, unions, parent–teacher organizations, civic groups, and fraternal organizations are highlighted. However, his data sources provide measures of membership in many other types of groups.

The survey questions that Putnam discusses in his research were asked every year for nearly two decades, which allowed him to compare trends in group membership, trust, and political participation. A summary of the responses to these questions reveals some interesting patterns (see Table 3.2) and permits some intriguing observations. For example, some forms of political participation were in decline, but voting appears to have rebounded. Less than half of all Americans voted in 1996, but by 2008 turnout was close to 1968 levels. We also see that political efficacy, as measured by the "officials don't care" question, dropped substantially during this period, as did support for the idea that government is run for the benefit of all. Is participation related to the decline in efficacy and increased cynicism about government?

The results in Table 3.2, while perhaps not too encouraging for American society, might offer a bit of support for one idea in the study—that some forms of political participation and efficacy were both low. There is more to concluding a study, however, than simply saying, "See, I was right (or wrong)!"

T A B L E 3.2   Trends in Political Participation and Trust, 1968–2008 (percent of survey respondents)

	1968	1976	1984	1988	1996	2000	2004	2008
Attend political meetings, rallies, or speeches	9	6	9	7	5	5	7	9
Work for a political party or candidate	6	5	6	3	2	3	3	5
Turnout for election	61	53	53	50	49	51	55	57
Government is run for the benefit of all	51	24	39	31	27	35	40	29
Officials do not care what people like me think	36	51	42	51	61	56	50	60

SOURCES: American National Election Study, various years, www.electionstudies.org; Federal Election Commission, http://www.fec.gov/pubrec/electionresults.shtml.

Analyzing the Results

As Table 3.2 indicates, political efficacy was higher in the 1960s than in subsequent years. In the past, more people believed government was run for the benefit of all, and more believed officials cared about people like themselves. Some forms of political participation (e.g., voting, working for candidates) also appear to have dropped slightly between 1968 and 2000. These trends are consistent with our hypothesis about the relationship between efficacy and participation. There was a minor rebound in voting and campaigning after 2000; however, this occurred during a period when people appeared to be even more cynical about politics than ever.

We can place these results in better perspective by adding in more years of survey data as they become available. We can also compare results in Table 3.2 to tests of hypotheses derived from Putnam's study. His question was whether membership in certain social groups led people to be more politically engaged and trusting of government. There are many ways we can test for this relationship. One is to look at trends over time. Figure 3.1 presents some preliminary results from trends in responses to GSS and ANES survey questions. We see that from 1974 to 1994, membership in church-based groups was in decline (albeit just slightly) and that trust in government dropped from more than 40 percent

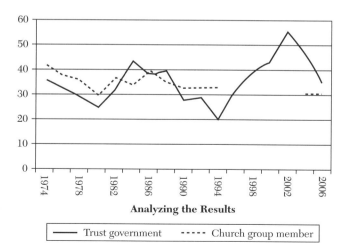

FIGURE 3.1 Trends in Trust and Church Group Membership, 1974–2006

SOURCE: Data for church group membership from General Social Survey; data for trust in government from American National Election Studies.

in 1974 to 20 percent in 1994. These results seem to support the basic hypothesis that social group membership is related to trusting government—but these results must be subjected to further analysis. It is not clear that long-term trends in trust were caused by trends in membership in social groups because the GSS did not ask the church group membership question between 1996 and 2002.

Another analytic technique is to see what impact other important variables have on the results. Our discussion of social capital theory suggests that membership in social groups has been in decline for some time. It also suggests that recent generations of Americans may be less likely to participate in church groups, service clubs, fraternal organizations, and other such social groups.

The data shown in Table 3.3 seem to bear this out. This table shows the percentage of people in different age cohorts who are members of no social groups, one or two groups, or three or more groups. Because we are interested in a person's generation more than their age, we list when they were born to better illustrate when they reached adulthood. As we can see, respondents who became adults in the 1950s (the "born 1925–1934" and "born 1935–1944" cohorts) were least likely to report that they were not members of any social group. In fact, 75 percent of each of these cohorts consisted of members of at least one group. In contrast, people who became adults in the 1990s and later (the "born 1975–1984" cohort) were least likely to report having any group memberships. They score lowest on the variable that we assume to be measuring social capital.

T A B L E   3.3   Levels of Social Group Membership by Age Cohort (percent of survey respondents)

Group Membership	Year Born					
	1925–1934	1935–1944	1945–1954	1955–1964	1965–1974	1975–1984
Not a member of any group	25	26	29	36	37	46
Member of one or two social groups	44	42	42	39	41	21
Member of three or more social groups	31	31	29	25	22	33

SOURCE: Authors' calculations from the General Social Survey 1972–2008 cumulative data file, http://www3.norc.org/gss+website/.

Of course, it is difficult to use these data to distinguish between generational effects (factors specific to an era when someone was growing up) and life-cycle effects (factors associated with how old someone is in any era),[9] but there is something going on here: The youngest generation of Americans has the lowest levels of social capital and some forms of political participation are in decline. This is consistent with Putnam's theory, but it does not "prove" it. There's much more that can be done to test how these things are related, but we now have a better grip on the problem than when we started.

We want to emphasize that by consulting multiple observations, you can gain perspective on the utility of the hypothesis test you have constructed. At the same time, other studies can provide a general check on your findings.

UNDERSTANDING THE RESULTS

Evaluating Concept Operationalization and Variable Measurement

Now that you have some research experience with the subject, rethink each step of the strategy in light of what happened. There is a big difference between thinking of a way to operationalize a concept and having it work as expected in the process of research.

The following are some questions for this project:

- Are the measures of political participation valid?

- How do we explain how participation increased after 2000, while efficacy declined and cynicism increased?

- Do the groups that we use as indicators of social capital all play the same role in building social connections among people? Is social capital simply an abstraction created by the researchers' interpretation of the data?

- How can we establish if there is a causal relationship between social group membership and political participation? Between group membership and trust in government? What is the direction of causation?

- Is the social capital argument something unique to America? Would we expect to find similar patterns in survey data from Europe and elsewhere?

We also need to consider how survey data might be biased. There is the problem of a person's state of mind when answering a question. Any number of factors can influence responses. For example, female interviewers might produce different responses from women than male interviewers would produce. It is useful to repeat studies at different times and in different places. If you ask college students to fill out questionnaires, be ready for the campus wit. The jokers, the devious, and the perverse can foul up a questionnaire in many ways.

Another possible form of interference with honest responses arises from respondents who feel there is something fishy about the project, the researcher, the questions, or the presumed confidentiality of the responses. An erstwhile sophomore once polled the faculty of a church-affiliated college about their personal use of marijuana. She did these interviews in person and assured the faculty that each response would be "confidential"—the data summaries were to be broken down by department and rank and the final paper would then be placed in the library. A junior faculty member in a small department, however, might conceivably have been wary of the promised confidentiality and might have been less than honest in responding to such an invitation to persecution—if not prosecution.

In dealing with people, science does not substitute for savvy.

Were the Measures Any Good?

Self-criticism is not a particularly welcome task, but in social science it serves two specific purposes. Obviously, it helps to reexamine a project after you have finished to be sure that the steps along the way are sufficiently well done to lead directly to the conclusion. Reexamination, however, serves another function. In dealing with something as slippery as the measurement of social phenomena, whatever is learned in the development and use of measures needs to be shared. A measure can look very impressive at the outset of an inquiry. The experience gained in actually using it, however, may turn up some unexpected weaknesses that, if stated as part of the results, can save someone else a lot of work.

In the case of Robert Putnam's social capital project, there are hundreds of different social groups in which people might report membership. In various writings, Putnam emphasizes a different mix of groups that matter—with church, sports, and arts clubs often cited as essential reservoirs of social capital.[10] The specific groups we decide to measure matter because different measures often produce different results. Although Figure 3.1 shows a decline in church-based memberships that corresponds with a decline in trust, questions from the same GSS surveys show that membership in other social groups was increasing (sports groups, school fraternities, and professional associations).

So which groups best cultivate the norms, networks, and connections that are essential to building the social capital needed for a democratic society? We need to know this in order to know which measures of group membership to use. If sports groups such as bowling leagues are important, we could ask people if they go bowling in leagues. But would responses to this question really measure how, or if, they interact with their fellow bowlers? Moreover, what does our measure pick up if many of the people who answer "yes" simply took a high school bowling class for P.E.?[11]

Remember that the idea behind social capital is that membership in groups leads to contacts with other people that build trust. A more convincing measure of the effects of social groups may be to ask people about the groups they join, and then also ask them how much time they spend meeting with members of the groups. This might give us a more direct measure of how social groups affect people. The GSS also includes questions about working as a volunteer and hours spent in certain group activities.

Does this criticism invalidate the measure? No; there is no such thing as a perfect measure. The point is to be able to defend your measure against likely alternatives. A researcher must have a good defense of how variables are measured and defined. Comparing findings obtained by different measures and diverse approaches to observation helps build understanding.

Can Statistics Be Trusted?

Assorted mystics throughout the ages have made much of examining the entrails of birds for portents and predictions of the future. Those skilled in statistical criticism are probably the modern heirs of this profession (particularly those who are adept at finding good news and bad news in any given statistic). That statistics do not provide, in and of themselves, precise answers to social inquiries surprises some and comforts others. It is easy to say that statistics can lie, or that they never quite get the whole message across and are therefore useless. But the question is, statistics (or measurement) compared to what? Compared to language concepts such as *more*, *less*, a *whole bunch*, or a *little bit*, statistics can be more precise. It is true that evidence involving numbers can be misleading—but words can mislead, too. Symbolic cues, loaded terms, imprecise language—all distort knowledge. The advantage of a scientific approach to observation is that biases can be more easily exposed because the specification of meanings and procedures is so explicit as to permit replication.

Of course, the wrong statistic can be used as easily as the wrong word, and science is no substitute for common sense. As you learn more about statistics, you will find that researchers typically use several statistical methods to summarize a situation, rather than relying on a single indicator, in order to compensate for the faults of any particular method.

How Do Your Findings Fit with Theories in the Field?

Although a simple experiment or inquiry might answer some puzzle that is on your mind, it might also relate in interesting ways to more general issues that are contained within theories on the subject. For example, it is mildly interesting to know how education influences people's judgments of presidential candidates. It is a lot more interesting to fit that finding to a whole set of ideas about the human condition. Can we indeed be trusted to select our own leaders? Does democracy really work? Is democracy well served when most citizens think officials do not care what they think? These are large theoretical perspectives, but theory does not have to be grand to be good. There are less global theories that explain key pieces of events.

Coleman, Putnam, and others who examine the effects of social capital begin their projects by discussing social and democratic theory, as well as previous research on the relationship between social groups and politics. They cite other writers, including de Tocqueville, who speak highly of the civic effects of social groups. De Tocqueville himself wrote in the 1830s that one of the most important aspects of American democracy was the widespread participation in voluntary associations—social groups that provided forums where people learned skills that made them better democratic citizens. This discussion highlights the relevance of Putnam's study and shows that declining interest in politics may have roots in deep social changes, rather than being due to our current crop of politicians or contemporary disdain for negative ads.

In evaluating the research we have presented in this chapter, refer to the general readings you have done. Also, if time allows, do some more investigations into what other people have found out about the link between social capital (or social group membership) and engagement with politics. Think about how (or if) democracy could be strengthened if more people interacted with each other in various social settings like charities, neighborhood organizations, sports clubs, and civic groups.

Scientific procedure is lifeless by itself. In the hands of an imaginative researcher it becomes a very useful tool, but the mind is a far more subtle instrument than any set of procedures for investigation. Where science as method ends, scientists as people take over.

A noteworthy scientist once commented that "science is observation," by which he meant to suggest that getting all wound up in the details of experimental and control groups, statistics, and the rest can obscure the purpose of scientific inquiry, that is, using your head to understand what is going on.[12] There is no such thing as the perfect experiment that explains everything about a given phenomenon. Be wary of people who say they have proven something—especially with "facts" based on statistics. Use the scientific method as a critical tool as well as a means of discovery. Seek out vulnerable assumptions and the limitations of evidence so that you know both what has been demonstrated and what has not.[13]

CONCEPTS INTRODUCED

Fact	Descriptive study	Social capital
Truth	Relational analysis	
Falsifiable statement	Operationalization	

QUESTIONS FOR DISCUSSION

1. One version of reality testing in science involves comparing some observed relationship with how the results would appear

if no relationship existed between variables. Look at Table 3.3 in this chapter. What would the data look like if there were no relationship between age cohort and the number of groups a person joins?

2. Do the social groups listed in this chapter reflect places where people develop "networks, norms, and social trust that facilitate coordination and cooperation for mutual benefit"? Do social networking sites such as Facebook serve the same role as traditional voluntary groups? Are unions or professional associations also groups that might build social capital?

3. Can you think of other ways of operationalizing participation in politics? Trust in government?

4. Do you think that respondents might give socially acceptable, if not entirely accurate, responses to questions about political participation? Is there any way to design a study that would avoid this problem of validity?

USEFUL WEBSITES

American National Election Study
www.electionstudies.org
Look up trends in political participation and attitudes about government. The website includes tables that cross-tabulate survey questions by various demographic traits.

General Social Survey
www3.norc.org/GSS+Website/
Look up responses to hundreds of questions about social and political attitudes. The website allows you to cross-tabulate responses to any questions in the online GSS codebook.

Bowlingalone.com
http://bowlingalone.com
This website offers promotional material for Robert Putnam's book and includes definitions of social capital as well as free access to data used in the book.

ENDNOTES

1. David Easton, *The Political System* (New York: Knopf, 1953), p. 53.

2. Robert D. Putnam, "Tuning In, Tuning Out: The Strange Disappearance of Social Capital in America," *PS: Political Science and Politics*, 28, no. 4 (1995), pp. 664–683. See also another article by Putnam, "Bowling Alone: America's Declining Social Capital," *Journal of Democracy*, 6, no. 1 (1995), pp. 65–78.

3. See James Coleman, "Social Capital in the Creation of Human Capital," *American Journal of Sociology*, 94: 95S–S120 (1988).

4. Another observer wrote that the "interpersonal transformation" that comes from being in groups "cannot be easily measured with the blunt instruments of social science." Jane Mansbridge, "On the Idea That Participation Makes Better Citizens," in *Citizen Competence and Democratic Institutions*, eds. Stephen Elkin and Karol Soltan (University Park: Pennsylvania State University Press, 1999), p. 291.

5. *Robert Putnam, Bowling Alone: The Collapse and Revival of American Community* (New York: Simon & Schuster, 2000).

6. Putnam, "Tuning In, Tuning Out," p. 666.

7. James Coleman, *Foundations of Social Theory* (Cambridge, Mass.: Belknap, 1990), p. 304.

8. The National Election Study Guide to Public Opinion and Electoral Behavior is online at http://www.electionstudies.org/nesguide/nesguide.htm. The General Social Survey cumulative file is online at: http://www3.norc.org/gss+website/. The GSS site allows you to do online analysis of the survey data. Data used in Robert Putnam's book can be found at http://bowlingalone.com.

9. The table presents "pooled" data from many annual GSS polls conducted from 1972 to 2008. Thus, a respondent in the "born 1945–1954" age cohort could have been surveyed any time between 1972 and 2008. A person in the "born 1985–1994" age cohort could have been interviewed more recently and been younger.

10. See the articles in note 2 of this chapter as well as Robert Putnam, *Making Democracy Work: Civic Traditions in Modern Italy* (Princeton, N.J.: Princeton University Press, 1993), and Robert Putnam, *Bowling Alone: The Collapse and Revival of American Community* (New York: Simon and Schuster, 2000).

11. The filmmaker Michael Moore noted that mass murderers Eric Harris and Dylan Klebold both took bowling at Columbine High School. Poking a finger at faulty causal reasoning, he suggested, in irony, that bowling might cause mass murder rather than social trust.

12. Robert Hodes, "Aims and Methods of Scientific Research," Occasional paper no. 9 (New York: American Institute of Marxist Studies, 1968), pp. 11–14.

13. For examples of questionable uses of science, see Daisie Radner and Michael Radner, *Science and Unreason* (Belmont, Calif.: Wadsworth, 1982).

4

Refinements

Hypotheses

Values and Hypothesis Formation

Of Theories and Models in Social Science

Relationships in Hypotheses

Levels of Relationships in Hypotheses

Variables

Operationalizing Concepts

Dimensions of Variables

> Enthusiasm and deep conviction are necessary if
> men and women are to explore all the
> possibilities of any new idea, and later experience
> can be relied on either to confirm or to moderate
> the initial claims—for science flourishes on a
> double programme of speculative liberty and
> unsparing criticism.
> —STEPHEN TOULMIN AND JUNE GOODFIELD

Developing a sense for the methodology of social science resembles learning to play pool. The basic elements of each are simple—in pool, a table with pockets, some balls, and a stick; in social science, hypotheses, variables, and measurements. Up to now, we have been looking at the simple shots: a hypothesis with two fairly obvious variables and observations of a relationship between them. In science, as in pool, the more elaborate strategies are variations on the basic technique.

A good pool player never tries a harder shot than absolutely necessary; so also with a social scientist. Likewise, professionals in both fields have had to invent techniques for minimizing error and getting around obstacles. In this chapter and the next, we discuss the elements in a slightly different order from previous chapters— hypotheses, variables, and then measurements—and explore some refinements of each. In other words, we will illustrate some bank shots in the corner pocket.

HYPOTHESES

Hypotheses do not spring full-blown from the intellect unencumbered by a web of thoughts and preferences. Like any other artifact of human behavior, a hypothesis is part of a mosaic of intentions, learnings, and concerns. Social scientists have debated long and hard over how to deal with this reality. Some have preferred that the researcher do everything possible to forget values and other biases in order to concentrate on "objectively" pursuing work in the name of professional social science. Others have insisted that ignoring the origins of a hypothesis is inefficient because it leads the researcher to ignore basic factors in his or her own approach to data.

There is another set of questions related to how hypotheses fit with such structures of thought as theories and models. The formation of useful theories is, after all, the end object of the exercise. Thus, the relations between theory and research require exploration.

Finally, there is the somewhat more mundane, operational matter of the kinds of relationships that can be built into hypotheses. These three topics—the roles of values, theories, and relationships in the formation of hypotheses—will be dealt with consecutively.

Values and Hypothesis Formation

The notion of **values** is in itself peculiar. Writers have often tried to come to grips with what a value is and how one value can be separated from another. The sticky part is that values are hard to isolate. I may believe in freedom, but not freedom to the exclusion of equality or freedom for certain kinds of behavior, such as theft. Values occur in webs of mutually modifying conditions.[1]

The confused self we all experience may often be seen acting out different sets of values at different moments, with a larger pattern visible only over a substantial time period. Still, there remains a kind of consistency to human character—enough so that we can, and do, make general estimates of the orientation to life that people have.

Social scientists generally have resolved the problem of the relation of values to research by recommending that one's value orientations be discussed when presenting a report of a project. Because values are such an intimate part of every step of forming a hypothesis, selecting measures, and evaluating conclusions, that is a fair request. The specification, however, cannot be an afterthought. The role of values has to be squarely faced at the outset of inquiry. If that is not done, you may not see what your values are doing to your research. For example, someone who is strongly religious might do research on dating habits involving questions that are premised on the immorality of premarital intercourse. The questions used might easily reflect such a bias and invite respondents to condemn a practice that they in fact approve.

Of Theories and Models in Social Science

The relationship of a hypothesis or an inquiry to theories and models of phenomena seems commonsensical. However, it becomes steadily more complicated when authors try to set down the relationship in writing.

We know what a **theory** is—a set of related propositions that attempts to explain, and sometimes to predict, a set of events. By now we also know what a hypothesis is. In a rough sense, a social science theory is a collection of hypotheses linked by some kind of logical framework.

In social science, the term *theory* connotes a degree of uncertainty about whether the understanding it offers is valid and correct. Theory means something quite different in the natural sciences. As examples, cell theory and the theories of evolution, relativity, and gravity are confirmed through repeated experiments, observation, and vast amounts of evidence. Few, if any, observations contradict the theory. They have the power to predict a wide range of natural phenomena. Natural science theories are factual statements of certainty. Unlike natural science theories, however, social science is built of tentative formulations of theory. Because human behavior is far more idiosyncratic than natural phenomena, theories about the social world are tentative, conditional, and phrased in terms of rough probabilities rather than certainty.

Two other terms enter into the discussion. Scientists use the term **model** to convey an implication of greater order and system in a theory. Models represent simplifications of reality in a manner that allows examination of key relationships. Economists, for instance, are heavily involved in efforts to create theoretical models in which unemployment, inflation, and other major variables associated with economic performance are related mathematically.

There are a good many theories in social science and, lately, some intriguing models. For those at the beginning of social scientific investigation, theory is best conceived of as a guide to inquiry—a way of organizing and economizing insight so as to avoid the trivial and isolate the significant.

In social science there are two general modes by which theory comes into play: inductive and deductive. **Induction** refers to building theory through the accumulation and summation of a variety of inquiries. **Deduction** has to do with using the logic of a theory to generate propositions that can then be tested.

The most popular image of science has researchers collecting bits of information through a gradual process of investigation and forming them into theories. The test then becomes whether the theory explains what is known about a phenomenon. The danger in accepting this simple view of science as induction is that the categories used to construct the inquiry may reflect an implicit theory. What is presented as induction turns out to be a hidden form of deduction. Scientific procedure is designed to reduce such biases by requiring that the propositions in a theory be put in falsifiable form, that is, that they be subject to testing through observation. As clear as that requirement would seem to be, social investigation is so value-laden and the tools for testing so limited that mistaken judgments can easily be made.

Deduction is becoming an increasingly common way of relating theory to research. Under pressure of attack from critics of the supposedly objective nature of social science, researchers are beginning to understand that deduction subtly enters into the formation of basic concepts commonly used in hypotheses. In American culture, the pervasive conditioning to a capitalist political economic system has led many political scientists, sociologists, and economists to take our system as the norm of the good society and to cast all nonmarket patterns of behavior into such negative categories as deviant, counterproductive, underdeveloped, and so on. Proceeding from such culture-bound assumptions, it becomes easier to argue that an individual who acts on motives other than material self-interest is "poorly adjusted," "irrational," or in need of treatment or confinement. The connotations of these labels are, in a real sense, deduced from a larger theory that implies the naturalness or rightness of one system of political economy. Yet these labels are presented as inductively determined scientific designations.[2]

Because deduction is a natural pattern of thought, it needs to be harnessed to scientific exploration. Very often deductions from theory provide the basic agenda of a field of inquiry. Established theories are guides to the solutions of many specific puzzles. The deductive route is well worth trying before starting anew in the task of explanation.

A good scientific inquiry can contain elements of both induction and deduction. The principal reason to keep these points in mind is to be conscious of self-delusion and of the ways others are misleading in their presentation of scientific findings.

Long before you are able to deal with the formation of theories, you will be a consumer of theory retailed by others. In utilizing research results, a precautionary question needs to be asked about the theory in terms of which the results are conceived to be meaningful. It is similar to the question about the values behind an inquiry, and it involves understanding the theoretical perspective from which an inquiry is undertaken. Never read a social science work without paying careful attention to the introduction and preface—therein usually lies the key to the author's commitments.

At the same time, do not be afraid to play with theoretical explanation as a guide to your own efforts. Science is democratic, and anyone can take an investigative potshot at a theory or try to extend it in new ways. By becoming aware of the predominant theories in a field, you can save some of your own time by borrowing their vision to see what the possible explanations of a phenomenon are.

Relationships in Hypotheses

Independent and Dependent Variables.   Not all variables are equal. If social science only managed to show that prejudice is associated with ignorance, youth with rebellion, and IQ with

For Example

Social Science Theory, Youth, and Democracy

Theory in social science involves conjecture, values, and uncertainty. Consider research on the health of democratic nations. Many scholars are interested in the conditions required for democratic nations to survive. They study citizens' attitudes about how democracy is working and how people think about nondemocratic forms of government.

A theory proposes that democratic nations require some baseline level of popular support for the core principles of democracy. Values are embedded in this sort of work: it is assumed, at least implicitly, that democracy is a good thing and that governments should be chosen via elections.

There is evidence of growing distrust of government in many established democracies. Younger people report higher support for being ruled by unelected "experts" and for military rule, compared with members of older generations.* For those who value democracy, this is problematic. Theory proposes that the public must support the selection of leaders with elections, yet studies show that the current generation of youth in many nations is more likely to support antidemocratic practices.

Hypotheses can be deduced from all of this. We might expect that as more people voice support for army rule, extremist, antidemocratic parties could receive greater support. Or if future generations of youth think like young people today, democratic practices may be endangered.

Of course, the theory as presented here could be wrong and in need of modification. It could be that distrust of government is healthy for democracy and that younger citizens may simply take longer to appreciate the virtues of democracy.

*David Denemark, Todd Donovan, and Richard G. Niemi. "Generations and Democratic Attitudes in Advanced Democracies." Paper presented at World Congress of the International Political Science Association, Madrid, Spain, July 10, 2012.

breastfeeding, social scientists would not have done as much as the culture has a right to expect. Are people prejudiced because they are ignorant or ignorant because they wear the blinders of prejudice? Which precedes the other? We almost asked, which causes the other, but did not because conclusive demonstrations of causation require elaborate procedures. The notion of independence and dependence in variables is a way of sneaking up on the question of causation without trying to go the whole distance.

An **independent variable** is one that influences another variable, called the **dependent variable**. For example, as heat increases, air can hold more water. Heat is an independent variable; the amount of water that can be suspended in the air is a dependent variable. What happens to the water depends on changes in temperature. If the air is soggy with moisture and heat goes down, water starts falling out of the air, which even social scientists refer to as rain.

In the example presented in Chapter Three, Putnam and others suggest that political participation depends on whether a person is active in voluntary social groups. Political participation is the dependent variable, and membership in social groups is the independent variable. Activity in social groups is supposed to build personal contacts and trust that give people the capacity to act politically. Thus, the hypothesis is that higher levels of activity in social groups lead to more political participation.

Reversal of the relationship you are considering is a good way to see whether a presumed relationship of dependence makes sense. Could voting or working on political campaigns cause people to join church groups or bowling leagues? Perhaps, but you would need a convincing theory that explains why the relationship would work in that direction. The theory of social capital gives us a persuasive argument for thinking that social activity precedes political activity.

Much of the time, there is nothing very tricky about the notion of independence and dependence. If we were looking at the relationship between education and voting decisions, it is pretty clear that voting cannot cause education. But there is something tricky about the fact that the relationship of independence and dependence is a figment of the researcher's imagination until demonstrated convincingly. Researchers *hypothesize* relationships of independence and dependence: They invent them, and then they try by observation and analysis to see if the relationships actually work out that way.

The question of independent and dependent variables can be more clearly understood when seen in the form social scientists are fondest of—tables. Tables are a method of presenting data, but behind a table is often a hypothesis with one (or more) independent variable and dependent variables.

Consider Table 4.1. Which is the independent variable? Which is the dependent variable? How would you reconstruct the hypothesis that these data support?

The two variables are income and political activity. These data illustrate which income groups dominate certain activities. What do these data say about the relationship between these two variables? The answer is that the wealthiest 10 percent of Americans

TABLE 4.1 **Political Activity Across Selected Income Groups (percent in each group who are active)**

	Annual Household Income			
	Less Than $20K	Between $30K and $50K	Between $75K and $100K	More Than $100K
Voted in last presidential election	56	69	82	82
Volunteered for neighbor-hood or civic group	32	36	39	55
Attended public meeting to discuss school or town affairs	30	45	53	63
Attended a political meeting or rally in past 12 months	10	16	22	33
Contributed more than $500 to nonreligious group	3	12	30	69
Percent of respondents in this income group	16	25	9	10

NOTE: Cell entries are the percent in selected income groups who report engaging in these forms of participation.

SOURCE: Authors' analysis of Social Capital Benchmark Survey national sample raw data file. Roper Center for Public Opinion Research, 2000. There were 3,003 respondents.

are far better represented among people who vote, who attend public meetings, and who contribute more than $500 to nonreligious groups. Larger numbers of poor and middle-class people are much less likely to vote, to attend meetings, or to make large contributions. A person in the highest income group is 2 times more likely to attend a town or school meeting, 3 times more likely to attend a political rally, and 23 times more likely to make large contributions than someone in the least affluent group. Income thus affects how people in each category participate in politics.

Therefore, income is the presumed independent variable and political activity is the dependent variable. To check on the assignment of the labels *independent* and *dependent*, reverse the hypothesis. Could the act of voting, for example, determine income? That does not make sense.

Table 4.1 illustrates the form in which tables are usually presented. The independent variable is listed across the top and the dependent variable down the side. By presenting tables in this standard fashion, researchers can locate the relationship without having to think about it. Nevertheless, it is a very good practice when look-ing at a table to formulate the hypotheses it is supposed to test. The author may have reversed the usual location of the independent and dependent variables for reasons of emphasis, style, or convenience.

Alternative, Antecedent, and Intervening Variables.   One of the central problems in developing strong hypotheses lies in understanding how variables stand in relation to each other. In hypothesizing connections between variables, you need to be aware of variables other than the ones you have selected that may be involved in producing changes in a relationship. Social scientists commonly refer to alternative, antecedent, and intervening variables.

All three terms have commonsense meanings. An **alternative variable** is an additional independent variable that influences changes in the dependent variable. An antecedent is something that comes before. For example, the antecedent of birth is concep-tion. To *intervene* means to come between. We will illustrate each of these concepts more precisely.

If one considers the variables that influence who contributes to political campaigns, several appear that might matter including gender, race, occupation, partisanship, and attitudes about govern-ment. These are alternative variables. Establishing the link be-tween income and contributing to campaigns (see Table 4.1) is useful nonetheless, though a complete account of why people do or do not contribute would have to include the influence of all the significant alternative variables. Income clearly does influence contributing, but gender and other variables intervene. If impor-tant variables are left out, the results may be meaningless or—as social scientists like to say—spurious. We shall return to the issue of spuriousness in the next chapter.

A classic illustration of an **antecedent variable** comes from the history of research on voting behavior. It became obvious from early surveys that more highly educated people tend to vote Republican. From that relationship, it could be implied that well-educated people are politically conservative. It turns out, however, that a powerful antecedent variable influences both the level of education and voting behavior: parental wealth. In fact, those who are highly educated tend to come from wealthier fami-lies, and wealthier families are more likely to vote Republican. What was being measured in the correlation of education with voting behavior was really the prior influence of parental wealth on the political preferences of their children.

As for **intervening variables**, suppose you are told that Hollygood Bread has fewer calories per slice than six other brands. The advertising leads you to assume that the independent variable is Hollygood's special formula for low-calorie dough. But you come to find out that the real reason for the difference is that the Hollygood company slices its bread thinner than the others. The dough actually has about as many calories as Sunshaft Bread or even Wondergoo. The thinness of the slice is the intervening variable between quality of dough and calories per slice.

To use a more elegant example, consider the relationship between education and social status. These two variables are positively associated; however, everyone knows of people who have modest educations but high social status. The reason might be that another variable enters the picture: occupational success.

To see how occupational success intervenes between education and status, think of the people you know who are poorly educated but who enjoy average status by virtue of their success at their job (group A). Now think of those who are well educated, successful, and high in status (group B). Think of yet a third group who are well educated but who have had lousy luck in the job market and have middling status by conventional standards (group C).

If you worked only with the relationship between education and status or that between occupation and status, rather than with all three variables, you would miss the point of the relationship between either pair. Group A would have you thinking that there is little connection between education and status, yet group B would make it appear that status and education go together like peanut butter and jelly. Meanwhile group C, just as educated as group B, has only average status. The same confusion would result from considering only the relationship between occupational success and status.

In general, well-educated people (group B) have higher status than poorly educated people (group A). Thus, it is demonstrable that education contributes to success. Occupational success, however, intervenes between education and conventional social status.

The way to avoid getting trapped by alternative, antecedent, and intervening variables is to do some thinking before formulating a hypothesis. Take the dependent variable and ask yourself what all the possible independent variables might be. If you want to explain why some people are fatalistic, think of all the variables that could influence such a state of mind. Possibilities might include the nature of their work, money troubles, unrequited love, background characteristics, the weather, or peer-group influences. In fact, most social phenomena—perhaps all social phenomena—are influenced by several variables. The point of worrying about alternative, antecedent, and intervening variables is not so much to discourage investigation of what interests you as to put it into perspective so that you do not confuse association with causation.

As another example, consider the argument frequently heard during election campaigns over the effect of state taxes on the employment rate. Critics of the cost of government are heard to argue that lowering taxes and spending will stimulate the state's economy by attracting businesses that don't like to pay taxes, thus adding new jobs and reducing unemployment. In Figure 4.1, we have indicated some of the antecedent, intervening, and alternative variables that might have an impact on a state's unemployment rate.

A careful sorting out reveals that many independent variables are involved, any one of which is likely to be more significant than the one hypothesized: state taxing and spending policies. In fact, the relationships among these variables are fairly complex. State political institutions such as direct democracy can cause

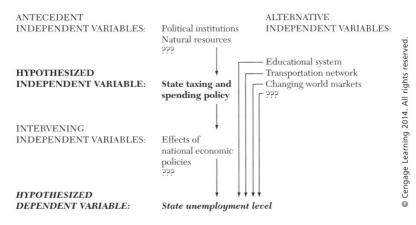

F I G U R E 4.1 Independent Variables Affecting Unemployment

lower taxes and spending through initiatives and referenda. Higher state taxes, however, insofar as they finance the educational system, may be the key to improving employment in a state.[3]

Once you recognize the variables that have a significant influence on a dependent variable, there are ways of separating out the influence of one variable from another. The simplest technique is to "control" for one variable by holding it constant while two others are tested for their relationship to each other. In the example of the connections between parental wealth, education, and voting behavior, one could select a sample of respondents with various levels of education from families of different wealth characteristics. If it turns out that highly educated children of wealthy families are predominantly Republicans and that highly educated children of poorer families are predominantly Democrats, you know that education is far less powerful than family wealth in shaping voting behavior. Tables 4.2 and 4.3 illustrate this hypothetical result.

As your methodological experience and sophistication increase, you will discover a host of techniques by which these connections can be sorted out. The first step in approaching the problem of sorting out variables is to understand the different levels of relationships that are built into hypotheses.

Levels of Relationships in Hypotheses

The most distinctive characteristic of a hypothesis as opposed to most ordinary sentences is the care with which each term is specified. We have seen that the selection of variables is a serious task in itself; so also with the relationships that are specified between variables. In order to stretch your imagination a little, it is worth considering systematically the possible relationships that can be expressed between two or more variables. They compose a

T A B L E 4.2   Relationship Between Education and Party Identification

Party Identification	Low Level of Education	High Level of Education	Total
Democrat	150	50	200
Republican	50	150	200
Total	200	200	400

T A B L E 4.3 **Relationship Between Education and Party Identification, Controlling for Wealth**

| Party Identification | From Poor Family | | | From Wealthy Family | | |
	Low Level of Education	High Level of Education	Total	Low Level of Education	High Level of Education	Total
Democrat	100	45	145	50	5	55
Republican	5	10	15	45	140	185
Subtotal			160			240

spectrum, and we will discuss briefly each of the relationships presented in Table 4.4.

The first relationship, the **null hypothesis**, is a rather ingenious creation. Remember that hypotheses are imagined relationships that are then put to the test. There is something to be said for positing no relationship and then testing to see if the null hypothesis can be disproved, that is, if it can be demonstrated that some relationship does indeed exist.

The utility of the null hypothesis is that the case is not prejudged—you are not caught defending a relationship specified beforehand. In addition to withholding commitment to a specific relationship, you are also leaving open the possibility that one of the more substantial relationships may characterize the connection between the variables. It may be that there is an **inferential** or a **correlative relationship** (or, simply, a correlation) that will emerge from the reality test. There may even be a **direct** or an **inverse relationship**, but those possibilities are left to emerge from the test itself.

The null hypothesis is admirably suited to a cautious strategy of social investigation. A null hypothesis can be disproven simply by demonstrating that there is any sort of association between two variables. Causation requires an enormous burden of proof and is at the opposite end of the relationship spectrum from the null hypothesis.

Inferential and correlative relationships can be tested as a preliminary to moving in on **causal relationships**. The lesser relationships, interesting in themselves, are also screening devices. If, in the example of the relationship between education and voter assessments of candidates, a correlation that is statistically significant can be

TABLE 4.4   Types of Relationships Between Variables

Relationship	Meaning
Null	No relationship is presumed to exist.
Inferential/Correlative	A relationship is presumed, but it is a relationship that deals with degrees of influence of one variable on another.
Direct/Inverse	A specific correlative relationship is presumed in which one variable has a predictable association with another—either one variable increases as the other increases (direct) or one variable increases as the other decreases (inverse).
Causal	Changes in one variable are presumed to result from variations in another.

demonstrated, then there is some reason to press ahead with the work of separating out extraneous sources of error that may be responsible for the correlation. That done, the alternative sources of causation may be tested to see if a causal hypothesis might be justified.

Several things need to be understood about the relationship of causation. First, it is probably the end object of social science to decide what causes what. Therefore, there is tremendous interest in establishing causality. Second, it is the most difficult relationship to deal with because it demands the highest burden of proof. To prove that A causes B, you need to demonstrate that:

1. A happens before B. Obvious, isn't it?

2. The occurrence of A is connected with the occurrence of B. This is obvious as well, but the connections of events are not always simple to discover. Some historians, for example, find a consistent link between the diets of reformers in the Middle Ages and the elaborateness of their visions. Joan of Arc, it is claimed, ate the wrong things, fouled up her digestive system, and so became a visionary and temporary heroine!

3. A causes B; there isn't some other variable (C) that eliminates the variation in B associated with A. This is where the going gets tough. It is always hard to eliminate all the possible influences, save one, in a situation. The time-honored technique in experimental social science is to select two groups of subjects, duplicate as closely as possible everything in the

environments of the two groups, and introduce the suspected causal variable to one group (the experimental group) and not to the other (the control group).

A classic example of the problems that arise in using the experimental–control group technique is the Hawthorne experiments, wherein one group of workers, the experimental group, was placed in a more pleasing physical environment for their assembly-line work. This experimental group consistently outproduced the control group, those working in the usual factory conditions. The trouble is that the increased productivity was later discovered to be mostly the effect of another variable—the special attention given the experimental group by the managers and experimenters themselves—rather than the physical surroundings. The experimenter had unknowingly introduced uncontrolled psychological factors: The two groups were differentiated by more than physical decor, thus violating the experimental–control group procedure and invalidating the results.

Most social scientists view the understanding of causation as the culmination of a long process of hypothesis formation and testing. The usual technique is to begin with a series of experiments to isolate the one variable that has the most obvious connection to the caused event. By this means, suspected sources of causation can be identified. The remaining logical steps usually demand a very high order of experimental elaboration. Consequently, beginners in the field are better off staying with relationships that can be more easily managed.

Because social science involves issues of great personal importance, it is hard to cultivate the habit of caution in hypothesis formation. Most beginners overstate their hypothesis, which leads them into measurement difficulties and the disappointments of an overworked conclusion. In trying to decide how strong a relationship to test for, give some thought to the measurements available as well as to the data resources within reach. A completely reported research experiment always contains the researcher's speculations about the larger ramifications of the results. But these are more palatable if the study itself observes sensible limits of hypothesis statement and measurement technique.

Establishing the logical relationships between variables in a hypothesis is, of course, a separate matter from testing to see if those relationships hold up. To see if a hypothesized relationship actually is borne out by observation, we need to move to the techniques of operationalization and measurement.

VARIABLES

Operationalizing Concepts

Early in our discussion of social scientific concepts, we saw how language begins with the problem of assigning names to different phenomena. Social scientific language consists of agreements between people that a given behavior is properly referred to by a given name. To operationalize a variable means essentially to fit the name used for a behavior to some specific way of observing and measuring that behavior. Variable operationalizing, in a way, reverses the process by which language is formed: Start with the name of the phenomenon that interests you, and work backward to find ways of tying that name to the specific behavior to which it refers.

The word *operationalization* makes the process discussed here sound special and expert, when in fact it is commonplace in everyday life. Late one evening, one of the authors of this book heard an argument in a saloon over which people are "better," Kentuckians or West Virginians. The discussion revolved around such items as the observation that one person's cousin's uncle's father-in-law was from Kentucky and he was no damn good. By comparison, however, it seems that the other person's former boss married a woman whose nephew was from West Virginia and he was born to be hanged! After several volleys of this sort, it became clear that the variable, the quality of Kentuckians and West Virginians, had been operationalized in terms of the affinity for criminal behavior of people living in those states.

As any science develops, the number of variable names that refer to carefully specified objects, events, or behaviors increases. There are now in the social sciences whole catalogues of variables operationalized in terms of specific behaviors and possible measurements.[4]

With a little luck, the variables that interest you have already been operationalized in a variety of ways. Even so, you need to know a number of techniques for operationalization in order to gain analytical flexibility and to be critical of what other people have done. In addition, you need to learn how to get around problems that arise when variables require forms of measurement that you do not have access to. There are two ways of dealing with a variable that, for some reason, is not amenable to operationalization: **substitution** and **division**.

Suppose your hypothesis is this: *The more educated people are, the more likely they are to be socialists.* Education is not hard to operationalize: The number of years spent in school tells you about exposure to formal education.

Whether people are socialists and, if so, how socialistic they are is quite another matter. The ideology called socialism brings together a complex of theories, versions of history, plans for action, and standards of good and bad. This bundle of things becomes all the harder to understand when it is realized that scholars of the subject have trouble agreeing on just what *socialism* means. Added to the difficulty of isolating a standard definition of socialism is the problem of dealing with unshared interpretations of the word on the part of the researcher, who is presumably trained in the formal ideological concept, and the sample survey respondent, who may think socialists are people who favor fluoridated water.

So it will not do to ask people, Are you a socialist and, if so, how much of a socialist? The answers to that question would generate some interesting data on self-perception, but the question would be too sloppy as a means of relating the respondents' attitudes to something as elaborate as socialist philosophy. Substituting for the variable *socialism* might solve some of those problems. Another variable could be found that pins down the attitudes involved more directly and deals with them in concrete terms. How about: *The more educated people become, the more they favor worker participation in management.*

The advantage here is that questions can be asked on a matter most people have an opinion about, and in terms that they can relate to. It does provide information relevant to the general hypothesis by picking up on an important element of socialist ideology, even though it is a substitution.

Division is another way of dealing with a difficult variable. Behavior is very seldom simple; it occurs in the context of related actions, attitudes, and dispositions. Often the variables social scientists deal with can be seen as combinations of behavioral ingredients. The variable *alienation*, for example, may be divided into four specific characteristics that are tied to the way people are thought to feel when they are alienated: normless, powerless, meaningless, and helpless. Attitude scales have been developed to try to measure each attitude ingredient of alienation. By combining measures of all four attitudes or feelings, you will have data that could respectably be said to have something to do with alienation.

Dimensions of Variables

Variables often have different **dimensions**. A psychologist measuring personality might come up with a classification of introverted and extroverted personalities. He or she might also come up with a characterization of aggressiveness–passivity on a scale from 1 to 10. These represent different dimensions of one variable: personality.

Public opinion usually is analyzed in terms of a variety of dimensions:

DIRECTION: The for-ness or against-ness of the opinion

LOCATION: Where on the scale from "for" to "against" is the opinion found?

INTENSITY: How strongly or weakly held is the opinion?

STABILITY: How changeable is it?

LATENCY: How close to the surface of the opinion structures is it?

SALIENCE: How important is that opinion in relation to others the person holds?[5]

All of these dimensions contain different measurement possibilities, and a variety of techniques are available to handle them. The direction of opinion requires only a specification that tells whether the opinion is on the "yes" side or the "no" side. Salience, on the other hand, allows an ordering of opinions from no salience to very great salience. Intensity of opinion suggests the possibility of scaling.

Before doing much work on a variable, think over which dimension you are looking at and what the other possible dimensions might be. Select those dimensions that are most promising in getting to the core of the variable. By looking at alternative dimensions, you can make choices as to which dimensions get to the crux of the variable and which dimensions can be measured by the means available to you. At the same time, an understanding of the different dimensions of a variable provides perspective on what has or has not yet been done to understand the variable.

One of the most persistent myths about science is that it can be entirely equated with measurement. As we have tried to make clear in this chapter, the real creativity in science goes into the operationalization of variables and the design of hypotheses. These very often require genuine creativity. Although measurement occasionally approaches an art form, it is more typically a matter of technique and the systematic application of mathematical concepts. As we shall see in the next chapter, measurement has its own logic and clever devices.

CONCEPTS INTRODUCED

Values	Alternative variable	Direct relationship
Theory	Antecedent variable	Inverse relationship
Model	Intervening variable	Causal relationships
Induction	Null hypothesis	Variable substitution
Deduction	Inferential relationship	Variable division
Independent variable	Correlative relationship	Dimensions of variable
Dependent variable		

QUESTIONS FOR DISCUSSION

To answer the questions that follow, examine the data represented in Tables 4.2 and 4.3. In this example, Table 4.2 is said to present the relationship between education and party identification. In Table 4.3, party identification for people from both poor and wealthy families is presented. Table 4.3 introduces a control for family wealth because party identification might also be associated with family wealth.

1. How does the original pattern seen in Table 4.2 change when we examine the two groups in Table 4.3?
2. Is the relationship between party identification and education affected by income?

3. What do the results in Table 4.3 indicate about the relationship between education and party identification?

4. Can you think of any logical explanation for the patterns displayed in the tables? What variable(s) is/are dependent? What variable(s) is/are independent? Why?

ENDNOTES

1. For an excellent discussion of how values relate to concepts and ideologies, see Michael Freeden, *Ideologies and Political Theory: A Conceptual Approach* (Oxford, U.K.: Oxford University Press, 1996), Part One.

2. See Murray Edelman, *Political Languages: Words That Succeed and Policies That Fail* (New York: Academic Press, 1977).

3. See, for example, Bryan D. Jones, "Public Policies and Economic Growth in the American States," *Journal of Politics* 52 (1990): 219–234. Jones finds that the overall size of the public sector is not associated with economic decline and that spending on education, highways, police, and fire protection is associated with employment gains and economic growth.

4. See John Robinson, Phillip Shaver, and Lawrence Wrightsman, *Measures of Political Attitudes* (San Diego, Calif.: Academic Press, 1999).

5. Adapted from Bradlee Karan, "Public Opinion and the New Ohio Criminal Code," The College of Wooster Symposium on Public Opinion and the New Ohio Criminal Code, July 9–30, 1973, pp. 6–8; and Vladimir Orlando Key Jr., *Public Opinion and American Democracy* (New York: Knopf, 1961), pp. 11–18. Key discusses variables in terms of their *properties* rather than their *dimensions*. With respect to public opinion, he uses the term *dimensions* where we have used *location*. In recent usage, the term *properties* has become a general name for all the characteristics of a variable: its measurements as well as its various substantive components, or dimensions, that have acquired the more specific meaning to which we refer.

5

Measuring Variables
and Relationships

> Not everything that counts can be counted, and not
> everything that can be counted counts.
> —A SIGN ON THE WALL OF ALBERT EINSTEIN'S OFFICE

S cientists basically measure three things: *variables, the chances that
data about variables are meaningful*, and *relationships between variables*. Each measurement task has distinctive approaches and statistical devices. As we look at tools used to accomplish these tasks,

remember that measurement almost always looks more precise than it really is.

The term *measurement* is used rather broadly in this chapter. For the first topic, the measurement of variance, we examine the kinds of measurement suited to different types of variables. Next, we look at techniques for describing the significance and representativeness of data obtained through scientific procedures. There are techniques for making fairly precise judgments about the chances that a set of data may be simply the result of a freakish sample rather than a meaningful measurement. In this connection, we show how sample surveys are constructed and discuss some common polling errors. Then, we present some ideas about measuring relationships *between* variables. The objective is to grasp the basic tools for reducing data about two or more related variables into a statistic that characterizes the relationship between the variables.

Conventionally, *measurement*, as a term, applies only to the first of these topics. The second concerns the problem of the significance and representativeness of data and uses probability, which is not, in the narrowest sense, a form of measurement. The third is often seen as a question of characterizing the association between things, rather than of measurement strictly speaking. Yet all three topics relate to the establishment of quantities of something: variance, significance, and association. Consequently, we have fit all three topics under the general rubric of measurement.

MEASURING VARIABLES: LEVELS OF MEASUREMENT

Measurement is a deceptive subject. At first, it seems simple— measurement answers the question, how much? This appears easy enough to answer when talking about length or weight but not so easy when considering such common fodder for social science as information levels, personal characteristics, feelings, and attitudes. The reason for the difficulty resides not so much in the matter of counting up units of things as in the nature of the things being counted. In measuring variables, for example, three considerations determine the level of measurement that can be attempted:

1. The properties or characteristics of the variable
2. The measurement technique appropriate to these properties

3. The levels of measurement that are possible in view of the variable's properties and available techniques

Consider, for example, a variable such as marital status. The variable refers to a classification according to a legal definition: single (with the subdivisions of unmarried, divorced, or widowed) or married (with perhaps the subdivision of monogamous or polygamous). In measuring someone's marital status, the property of the variable dictates that you cannot do more than categorize—it is not possible to say that someone is very much married or very little married. In the eyes of the law, you either are or are not married. Given such a property, the variable *marital status* does not call for a very fancy measurement technique.

The variable *intelligence* poses different possibilities for measurement. The **properties** of the variable do not limit consideration to mere classification: The variable has properties that imply larger and smaller amounts. This is where technique comes in. People have puzzled for centuries over how to measure intelligence. Efforts have included tests such as the sense to come in out of the rain—in which case intelligence can be measured in two categories: those who do and those who do not have the sense to come in out of the rain. Research marches on, however, and we have the intelligence quotient (IQ) test. The IQ test gives us a reading on how well people can answer certain kinds of questions that are thought to have something to do with intelligence. This advance in technique permits fairly detailed gradations between the low and high ends of a scale associated with certain kinds of intelligence.

Measurement comprises an area of research all by itself. Researchers keep trying to develop measurement techniques that can explore all the properties of important variables. In order to systematize our understanding of various kinds of possible measurements, scientists have come up with a classification of four levels of measurement:

1. Nominal
2. Ordinal
3. Interval
4. Ratio

In Figure 5.1, the characteristics of these levels are explored. The **nominal** level does not quite seem like measurement; it refers to classifications of things. Take nationality for an example. If

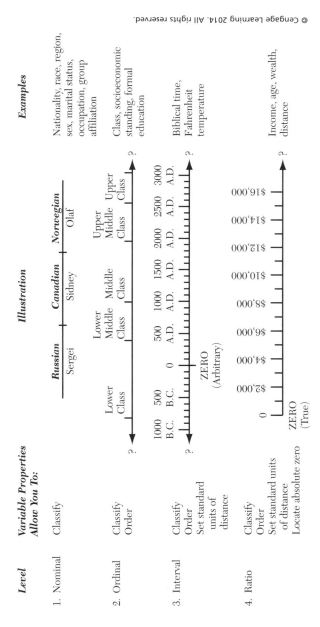

FIGURE 5.1 Levels of Measurement

Sidney is a Canadian and Sergei is a Russian, we have said something about the properties of each person in relation to a variable called nationality. That is measurement, but not very fancy measurement. We cannot rate Canadians above Russians (except according to some other variable, such as fondness for hockey—and even then, it would be close). Therefore, classification, or nominal measurement, is all that the properties of ethnicity as a variable allow.[1] Nominal measurement, crude as it is, pops up frequently in social science, as the examples listed in Figure 5.1 indicate: race, region, sex, occupation, and so on.

If the properties of the variable allow ordering as well as classification, the **ordinal** level of measurement can be attempted, provided the techniques are available. At this level, we can think in terms of a continuum, that is, an array that indicates variation, as opposed to simple classification. Class is one illustration, and socioeconomic standing is another. We can say that Alphonse is upper class, while Mack is lower class. These are classifications, but they are arranged in such a way as to link them on a continuum from lower to higher. Similarly with formal education: Deborah has a Ph.D., Fiona a high school education, and Ian a grade school certificate. A Ph.D., however, is not the same "distance" from a college degree as a high school diploma is from a grade school certificate. Ordering, yes; standard distance, no.

The specification of distance or, more generally, the amount of variation between cases, is an important step up in the realm of measurement. Distance affords a decided increase in the sophistication with which a variable can be measured and related to other variables.

If standard distance can be established, the next level of measurement enters the picture: **interval** measurement. Here, units can be identified that indicate how far each case is from each other case. That is reasonable, but there remains one of those technicalities that causes confusion of the mind. It has to do with absolute zero on a scale of measurement.

Interval measures do not have a **true zero**. What is a true zero? And what good is it? In the example of biblical time, the year zero does not mean that nothing happened before then. We do not really know where true zero is in history. Zero was established in relationship to the life of Christ for religious reasons and serves as a convenient reference point for counting forward and backward. The same is true of Fahrenheit temperature. You know that 0 degrees Fahrenheit does not represent a true zero because 23 degrees below zero is a lot colder than 0 degrees.

A **ratio scale** does have a true zero. A ratio scale such as *distance* is different from an interval scale because, for example, in a ratio scale, zero inches means just that—no distance at all. There cannot be less than zero distance, or less than zero weight, or less than zero bananas. That tells you the formal difference between a true zero and an **arbitrary zero**, or one that is made up for the sake of convenience.

But what good is a true zero? The answer has to do with what can be said in comparing observations on a ratio or an interval scale. If Hardy weighs 200 pounds and Laurel weighs 100 pounds (ratio scale), we can see that Hardy is twice as heavy as Laurel. But if the temperature is 50 degrees Fahrenheit on Monday and 25 degrees Fahrenheit on Wednesday (interval scale), can we really say that it was twice as hot on Monday as on Wednesday? You can try to get away with it, but you really should not because a comparison of that kind requires a true zero. You need to know what the total absence of heat is when determining whether one day was twice as hot as another. Without a beginning point, distances can be established, but not ratios.

The reason for knowing these distinctions has to do with the kind of relationships that can be established statistically within and between variables. The job is to avoid comparing apples and oranges. Statistics enter this text only in the form of ideas behind numbers—the arithmetic and the finer points of various statistical operations are left to more technical writings. Here we content ourselves with some simple points (simple as statistics go). Roughly speaking:

- Nominal measurement allows statistics that relate to the frequency of cases in each classification (e.g., ethnicity: 10 Canadians, 3 Russians).

- Ordinal measurement allows statistics that describe the way the cases are ordered with respect to a variable (e.g., education: grade school, high school, college).

- Interval measurement permits comparisons of quantitative differences among cases on a scale (e.g., time: 1950, 1990).

- Ratio measurement permits comparisons of absolute distances between cases (e.g., money: $10, $20).[2]

Because these levels of measurement determine how relations between variables can be approached, it is essential to figure out the appropriate level of measurement for each variable before proceeding with research. We will see the significance of levels of measurement spelled out in more detail as we turn to the problem of measuring variable relationships in the form of correlations.

MEASURING THE SIGNIFICANCE AND REPRESENTATIVENESS OF DATA: PROBABILITY, SAMPLING, AND PROBLEMS IN POLLING

We now turn to topics that fit together not so much because of their general connection with measurement but because they all relate to understanding the strengths and weaknesses of data that are to be analyzed. The topics are *probability*, *sampling*, and *problems in polling*. Public opinion polling provides a useful arena for examining sampling and probability, but these topics also have much wider applications in social science. Polling is but one of many ways to collect data systematically.

Probability

To get hold of the statistical tools basic to scientific research, we need to become familiar with a new concept: **probability**. Probability occupies a far more important place in social science than the amount of space devoted to it in this book would suggest. Probability constitutes nothing less than a fundamental of the scientific perspective. To understand why is to come to grips with some particularly ornery habits of the human mind.

Probability refers to the likelihood or chance of something occurring. Intuitively, we might compute probabilities about the chances of passing a course, the prospects for getting a date, or the odds of a team winning a game. That *Roget's Thesaurus* lists so many alternatives for the word *probability*—*likelihood*, *hazard*, *contingency*, *chance*, and others—indicates the importance of the concept in our language. It is important to remember that in social science, probability means something different than luck, fortuity, or fate. It is a much more systematic assessment of the odds that something might occur.

We began by saying that science is useful to human beings as a way of coping with the uncertainties of life. By forcing ideas and notions out of the head and into the arena of empirical observation and by testing them, we gain knowledge about the world. The scientific establishment is built on the power provided by this effort to escape the insecurity of uncertainty about our surroundings. It is characteristic of scientific knowledge, however, that it is rarely cast in stone. Often explicitly and always implicitly, scientific generalizations are probabilistic because observation enables only limited insight.

Science is the refinement of chance far more often than the discovery of certainty. Indeed, social scientists often discuss their findings in a language that expresses the possibility of being wrong. We worry about the odds that a set of results reflects an inaccurate sample or that another researcher would find results that are different from ours. Formally, we rarely speak of social science as conclusively proving anything.[3] Rather, we speak of the probability that a hypothesis is supported by the available evidence.

Sampling

As an illustration of the way probability is built into social science, we consider two special applications of probability statistics: determining the statistical significance of an array of data and constructing representative samples of larger populations. A sample is a subset of a larger population. We often cannot measure an entire population, so we find a smaller sample of the population to observe. We use probability to specify the odds that observations from a sample reveal something more than a chance relationship between variables. If the data come from a faulty sample or if they represent merely a freak combination of cases, then the results cannot be said to tell us anything conclusive about the relationship between the variables. It is important to know that, and probability statistics provide some clues.

The first usage of probability concerns the representativeness of a sample drawn from a larger population. Given the size and characteristics of a sample, what is the probability that we can infer from a sample of some specific characteristics of the larger population? This form of probability underlies public-opinion polling. Pollsters often try to estimate the percentage of the public that intends to vote for a specific candidate. In attempting to characterize the behavior of a huge group of people, it is, in most cases, impossible to survey everyone. Selecting the smallest, most representative possible sample is the key to efficiency in polling. Probability statistics are used to estimate the chances that a sample is representative.

The second application of probability involves estimating the likelihood of a set of observations occurring by chance. If there is only 1 chance in 100 that the results we are seeking would have occurred randomly, then the pattern is quite significant. A pattern of data linking two variables (say, income and education) that has a chance of occurring randomly 1 time in 100 tells us something useful. Without probing the mathematics, we would refer to this result as significant at the 0.01 level. Significance statistics are derived by combining the number of observations in the sample, the amount of variation in the variables, and the magnitude of the observed relationship. The most likely random distribution of results would show the same number of cases in each cell of a table; the least likely would have all the cases in one cell.

Establishing the **level of significance** of the results constitutes an important test of the hypothesis. Results demonstrating that all upper-income people are highly educated and that all lower-income people are poorly educated are most unlikely to occur by chance. The independent variable observably has a very strong impact on the dependent variable. There is very likely a correlation between income and education in the population. Significance tests tell us that, under certain conditions, the probability that our hypothesis is right (or wrong).

In its most basic form, significance tells us "whether or not a certain relationship … is worth further thought—whether it might repay additional research effort."[4] Some social scientists will deal only with data significant at the 0.01 level, whereas others accept 0.05 as the cutoff—meaning that there are 5 chances (as opposed to 1 chance) out of 100 of the observed relationship occurring by chance. The significance level is commonly noted as part of a research report, which helps in evaluating results.

The two uses of probability we have been discussing are related: The first deals with whether the sample is representative, and the second concerns the chances that the results are meaningful. Loosely stated, the questions become, is the sample representative? (inference) and is the pattern of results likely to have occurred by chance? (significance).

A representative sample provides a sound basis for inferring the level of support for a hypothesis, especially if the pattern of observations is statistically significant. A poor sample, however, will make for poor inferences, whether or not the pattern of data is significant. A sample drawn according to probability theory is known, not surprisingly, as a **probability sample**.

There are two general techniques used in sampling: stratification and random sampling. **Stratification** involves trying to reproduce a large population by representing important characteristics proportionately in the sample. If we tried to determine a community's attitude toward drinking by interviewing a sample of customers at a local saloon, that sample would overrepresent one segment of the public in terms of a characteristic vital to the issue under consideration. Teetotalers do not hang out in saloons. Therefore, we would have to select the sample in such a way that teetotalers have a chance of being included.

If the stratification method were used to select a sample for determining voting behavior in an election, we would try to have a sample that reflected proportionately the larger population—at least in terms of such significant independent variables as class, region, and education. The stratification (proportionate sampling of certain characteristics of voters), however, must be limited to a relatively small number of characteristics. Otherwise, in order to fill out the sample with representatives of all the variables in the proper proportion, we might wind up spending valuable resources trying to find people with highly unlikely combinations of characteristics.

Random sampling depends on selecting at random a sufficient sample of the population such that there is a high probability of reproducing the essential characteristics of the total population. The likelihood of representativeness increases in predictable fashion as the size of the sample grows. For example, if we interview five randomly selected people out of a national population of 210 million, the chances are not so good that they are truly representative—there would be a very high margin of error. With each increase in the size of the sample, provided the people are selected randomly, the margin of error decreases.

For any size of population, it is possible to determine mathematically the probability that a given sample size will generate a specified margin of error. The margin of error drops drastically with the increasing size of the sample, up to a point at which further increases in sample size reduce the margin of error very little. This is the point that indicates the most economical sample size. By doubling or tripling the sample size beyond this point, or even multiplying it by 10, relatively little reduction of error can be achieved.

One major problem with random sampling is that in order to interview all of those who are selected, the interviewers have to disperse their efforts and seek out respondents in all corners of the total population. Most scientific sampling uses both stratification and randomization. For example, in a national sample, one might select representative urban areas and representative rural areas (a form of stratification) and then draw a random sample within those target areas.

Telephone sampling, although it contains a bias against those who have no phones, has become an increasingly popular technique now that computers make it possible to do random digit dialing within specific telephone exchanges. Evolutions in communications technology are introducing new biases to phone sampling, however. Pagers, beepers, and answering machines are hooked up on many telephone exchanges. Annoyance with heavy telemarketing efforts might be boosting refusal rates for survey researchers. Good phone samples may still be drawn, but costs are increasing as researchers act to minimize these new biases. Also, the Internet creates new possibilities for establishing panels of respondents who can be polled on important questions.

For their surveys of American opinion, major academic, commercial, and media polls (such as Pew Research, Gallup, CNN/Opinion Research, CBS/*New York Times,* Reuters/Ipsos, ABC News/*Washington Post*, and NBC/*Wall Street Journal*) use a stratified random sample so as to eliminate, among other problems, the inconvenience of interviewing a randomly selected sheepherder in a remote section of Nevada. The sample size is typically about 1,500 persons. At this size, the margin of error is about 3 percent at the 0.05 level of significance. What this means is that 95 samples out of 100 should produce a measure of the opinions of the actual population, within a range of plus or minus 3 percent. So if 49 percent of the actual population plans to vote Democrat, then 95 out of 100 samples would produce estimates ranging from 46 percent to 52 percent.[5]

Problems in Polling

Major media firms have had fairly impressive records of achievement when using samples of this kind to predict presidential elections, in part because they have been lucky in not drawing a "way-out" sample, one of the 5 in 100, and in part because they do stratify their samples somewhat to avoid the weird sample that might occur if simple random sampling were used. This does not mean their predictions are perfect. Surveys conducted by the Pew Foundation demonstrate notable differences in telephone samples drawn exclusively via landlines versus those that include cell phones and landlines. Landline-only samples underestimated support for Barack Obama in 2008, and landline-only samples estimated 5 percent more support for Republican congressional candidates in 2010 compared with samples that included cell phones.[6]

Prediction is also difficult if you are trying to use a sample to represent real values that are nearly indistinguishable from each other. On election night in 2000, data from exit polls used by the major networks twice led them to predict the wrong outcome in Florida. This led them to declare that Al Gore, rather than George W. Bush, was elected president. One problem in Florida was that the election there was so close—essentially a 49 percent to 49 percent tie.[7] For the networks to call Florida in favor of Gore, their polling data must have shown that he had a lead of at least 1 to 2 percent to be confident their prediction was beyond the margin for error.[8]

The 2000 Florida exit polls failed by estimating, with confidence, that Gore received more votes than Bush. This does not mean that the prediction about who won was totally wrong. Exit polls identify whom voters thought they voted for on election day. A plurality of Florida voters may have tried to vote for Gore on election day—but voter error, equipment failure, and overseas ballots that were counted after the election muddled the final count and probably cost Gore the presidency.[9] Even with all these things accounted for, the polls overestimated the proportion of voters who believed they had voted for Gore. The true margin between Gore and Bush was still less than 0.05 percent. A perfectly representative sample should have shown this and led the networks to realize it was too close to call.

Another way of understanding sampling is to consider how poor samples lead to faulty conclusions. Bad samples have led to some major mistakes in forecasting presidential elections. A now-defunct publication, the *Literary Digest*, made itself famous by surveying millions of voters per election and forecasting (accurately) the presidential elections of 1924, 1928, and 1932. The accuracy of these forecasts was attributed by many people to the sheer size of the sample. The *Digest*, however, mailed surveys to people drawn from lists of car and telephone owners—a method that ran a serious risk in the 1920s and 1930s of underrepresenting the less affluent. After surveying more than 2 million voters in 1936, the *Literary Digest* inferred from its sample that Alf Landon would defeat President Franklin D. Roosevelt, with Landon getting 57 percent of the vote. President Landon? It did not happen. Landon received only 36 percent of the vote in the election. It should be stressed that a large sample will not necessarily compensate for unrepresentativeness.[10]

Techniques such as stratified random sampling have greatly improved the reliability of polls; however, candidates and interest groups sometimes conduct surveys that replicate the mistakes of the *Literary Digest* polls. Consider the data shown in Table 5.1. During the 1992 presidential campaign, independent candidate Ross Perot's organization mailed out surveys in *TV Guide* magazine and asked readers to mark their ballots as they watched a televised address by the candidate. Responses were then mailed back to Perot's organization. Yet when another group drew random probability samples and respondents were given the same questions, results differed substantially from those reported by the Perot organization.[11] The Perot data suffered from the error of **sample bias**; no real attempts at randomization or stratification

T A B L E 5.1   **Taxing and Spending: The Effects of Sample Bias (percent of respondents)**

Question 1: Do you believe that for every dollar of tax increase there should be $2 in spending cuts with the savings earmarked for deficit and debt reduction?

	Yes	No	No Answer
TV Guide Mail-In Response	97	na	na
Yankelovich National Sample	67	18	15

Question 2: Should laws be passed to eliminate all possibilities of special interests giving huge sums of money to candidates?

	Yes	No	No Answer
TV Guide Mail-In Response	99	na	na
Yankelovich National Sample	80	17	3

SOURCE: "H. Ross Perot Spurs a Polling Experiment (Unintentionally)," from pp. 28–29 by David M. Wilbur, in *Public Perspective*, vol. 4, no. 4 (1993). Reprinted by permission of The Roper Center for Public Opinion Research.

were made. Consequently, this poll could not be presented as a credible representation of public opinion.

It should be noted that other sources of error creep into survey research in addition to the representativeness of the sample. A researcher may have selected a highly representative sample, but his or her instruments of measurement may elicit misleading answers. Common sources of error include those presented in Table 5.2.

Beyond these obvious kinds of error, some errors arise from the difficulty of being sure you are measuring what you think you are measuring. An example would be a question developed out of an interest in understanding people's personal sympathies for the poor: Do you approve or disapprove of poor people stealing bread when they are hungry? Someone who has enormous sympathy for the poor might say, "I disapprove," because that person, while sympathizing with the poor very strongly, also has enormous respect for law and order. Note that the question is not meaningless; the error comes from attributing an inappropriate meaning to the responses. The question taps another variable, *respect for law and order*, in addition to the one intended, *attitudes toward the poor*.[12]

Added to errors arising from sloppy measurement are errors introduced by the statistical procedures used to characterize the data. Statistics always distort reality to at least a small degree—

T A B L E   5.2   Common Sources of Question Wording Error

Error	Example
Ambiguous questions	Do you think we ought to strive for peace or for a strong defense?
Symbolically loaded questions that elicit biased answers	Do you think unborn children have a right to life? Do you think pregnant women should have the right to choose an abortion?
Difficult questions beyond the information level of the respondent	Do you approve or disapprove of the regulation of the financial industry contained in the Dodd/Frank bill passed by Congress?
Response alternatives unsuited to the subject of the question	Do you feel better or worse about the future?
Questions that include more than one issue	Are you more likely to favor a candidate who supports tax cuts and a strong defense or one who has a pleasing personality?

that is why statisticians prefer using several techniques to characterize data so as to hedge against the bias of a single procedure.

MEASURING RELATIONSHIPS BETWEEN VARIABLES: ASSOCIATION AND CORRELATION

Establishing a degree of **association** between two or more variables gets at the central objective of the scientific enterprise. Scientists spend most of their time figuring out how one thing relates to another and structuring these relationships into explanatory theories.

As with other forms of measurement, the question of association comes up frequently in normal discourse, as in "Like father, like son"; "If you've seen one, you've seen 'em all"; or "An orange a day keeps the scurvy away." In measuring the degree of association between variables statistically, scientists are merely doing what science is famous for: being rigorous and precise about a commonplace activity.

Association can sometimes be characterized in simple ways. The effects of one variable on another can be described in words or by statistics. For example, "People who use Crust toothpaste have fewer cavities" is a statement that presents a relationship between an independent variable, *brushing with Crust*, and a dependent variable, *number of cavities*.

Descriptive statistics such as the median, the average, and the standard deviation can be employed effectively to specify association. For example, in our discussion of election systems and voter turnout in Chapter Two, the percent of voters participating in each nation was averaged for three categories of election system (see Table 2.2). This permits analysis of the effect of election systems on turnout. Percentage differences are also handy comparative instruments. For example, our discussion of the relationship between social group membership and generations in Chapter Three (see Table 3.3) showed that 46 percent of people in the youngest age cohort were not members of any voluntary associations. If there was no relationship between age cohort and group membership, we would expect that 46 percent of people in every age cohort did not join any groups. This is not the case. Just 25 percent of people in the older cohort had no group memberships—a 21 percent difference.

At this point, we might ask if 21 percent is a big enough difference to say there is a relationship between age cohort and group membership. In this case, the answer is yes. Measures of association and correlation provide us the tools to answer such questions.[13]

Measures of Association and Correlation

For certain applications, statisticians have developed more sophisticated tools for specifying relationships between variables: measures of association and correlation. Variables measured at different levels (see page 82) require that different statistics be used to test for association. The result is an alphabet soup of tests customarily designated by letters of the Greek alphabet, for example, *chi* and *rho*. All of these tests tend to share a common logic.

Measures of association and correlation are usually approached as a statistical matter; here we concentrate on the ideas behind them. Our discussion should help you recognize a correlation statistic when you see one. To understand the arithmetic and the limiting assumptions, you may consult a statistics text.

The essential idea of **correlation** is to describe statistically the direction and strength of association between variables. Assuming all other conditions are equal, measures of association summarize the movement of two variables in relation to each other.

Correlation analysis allows you to capture in a single statistic both the direction and the amount of association. **Direction** refers to whether the association is positive or negative. A positive correlation exists when, as variable *A* increases, variable *B* also increases. That is, variable *A* goes up as variable *B* goes up (or vice versa). A negative correlation exists when, as variable *A* changes, variable *B* changes in the opposite direction. In the case of a negative correlation, as *A* increases, *B* decreases (or, as *A* decreases, *B* increases).

For example, there is a positive correlation between the quantity of helium in a balloon and the rate at which the balloon rises. There is a negative correlation between the rate of rise and the weight attached to the balloon. The positive/negative direction is expressed by a plus or minus sign before the correlation figure.

The strength or amount of correlation is expressed by the size of the number on a **scale** from 0 to +1.00 or −1.00. The scale is illustrated in Figure 5.2. Thus, correlation statistics provide simple indexes of relationships between variables.

As with all statistics, the appearance of precision can be misleading; the mathematics behind correlation statistics involves assumptions that require careful thought. In addition, the variety of techniques by which measures of association are computed causes the results to deviate slightly from the reality of the data.

An understanding of the general techniques by which correlation operates will allow you to see some, though not all, of the problems. Nevertheless, in the imperfect world of measurement, these statistics are valuable tools.

The techniques for computing measures of association vary with the level of measurement used. If two variables are measured on a nominal scale (classification only), there is less that can be done to characterize association than would be the case with two variables measured on an interval scale. In fact, there are correlation techniques available for every level of measurement, and we describe generally how they work.

Nominal-Level Association Nominal measurement, involving only simple classification, is low-grade stuff and the measure of association appropriate to it really does not deserve to be called correlation. The **contingency coefficient** is a statistic that summarizes

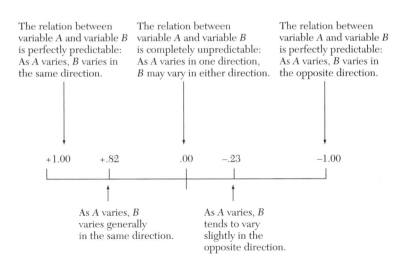

FIGURE 5.2 The Scale of Correlation

how far the actual distribution of data deviates from a distribution in which one variable is associated with no change in the other.

Suppose a researcher wishes to test the proposition stated in the title of an old Steve Martin movie, *Dead Men Don't Wear Plaid*. The researcher decides to check on the frequency of plaid-wearing among dead men as well as living men to see if being deceased really does make a difference—speaking sartorially. The researcher views a random sample of 20 living men and checks the local funeral parlor for 20 deceased males. If it turns out that men wear plaid just as often when they are alive as when dead, then Martin's hypothesis is not worth much.

Table 5.3 presents a set of results showing no association between wearing plaid and being dead or alive. This is what we might see if there were no association between the two variables. The figures show that 24 plaid-wearing men are evenly divided among the living and the dead. Similarly, 16 nonplaid-wearing men are also as likely living as dead. In this case the contingency coefficient would be zero.

But suppose we actually observe a distribution like the one shown in Table 5.4. What if there were differences in the amount of plaid-wearing among dead men as opposed to living men? How could this be expressed in precise statistical terms?

The contingency coefficient is computed by comparing a distribution of (1) what we would expect to see in a table if there were no association (Table 5.3) to (2) what we actually might observe (Table 5.4). The results can be expressed as either a chi-square (pronounced *kye-square*) statistic or a contingency coefficient. Because chi-square has no upper limit, for the sake of interpretation it is often converted into a statistic such as the contingency coefficient, which has larger values reflecting greater association. If, in fact, the distribution shown in Table 5.3 was found,[14] then the contingency coefficient would be 0.41 and the

T A B L E 5.3   Frequency of Plaid Wearing

Pattern of Clothing	Condition of Men	
	Living	Dead
Plaid	12	12
Nonplaid	8	8

T A B L E 5.4   Observed Incidence of Plaid Wearing

Pattern of Clothing	Condition of Men	
	Living	Dead
Plaid	5	14
Nonplaid	15	6

chi-square would equal 8.12. These statistics point to an association between mortality and clothing—but it is not the one suggested in the movie title. It appears that a greater proportion of dead men wear plaid than living men.

In more systematic language, this sort of distribution indicates some association between being deceased and wearing plaid. The contingency coefficient is used to characterize the association between nonorderable, nominal-level variables.[15] This measure ranges from −1.0 to +1.0. Remember, a minus statistic indicates that as one variable increases, the other decreases (or vice versa). A plus statistic means that the variation is in the same direction for both variables. On a scale from −1.0 to +1.0, .41 would be a modest level of association. We could consult a statistics text to determine if the chi-square statistic indicates that the association is statistically significant.

Ordinal-Level Correlation   *Ordinal* means order. This characteristic supplies the basis for statistics that can be computed at the ordinal level. When the possibility exists of ordering as well as classifying the categories in the variable, establishing genuine correlation becomes possible. What can be done is to compare the ranking of cases according to their ordering on two variables. An illustration will help.

Imagine a group of 160 children being evaluated for placement in ski school classes. The instructor, a systematic person, believes that children from larger families, having learned from their siblings, are better skiers. The children are evaluated and placed into groups according to their ability from best to worst: expert, advanced, intermediate, and beginner. The instructor has two ordered classifications to work with: skiing ability, ordered in terms of expert, advanced, intermediate, and beginner, and family size, ordered in terms of huge, large, mid-sized, and small. The hypothesis she wishes to test is that there is any association between family size and skiing ability.

If the hypothesis were true, the data would show a certain pattern. As family size increased, skiing ability would increase. The group of children coming from huge families would be heavily populated with experts, and the small family group with beginners. Suppose she found the distribution presented in Table 5.5.

The relationship is not crystal clear from the data, but we can see that there is a pronounced tendency for kids from huge families to cut turns more sweetly than their peers from small families. Now we need a statistic that helps nail down the degree of association. Goodman–Kruskal's gamma, among other similar statistics, uses an interesting logic to summarize the degree of association. Gamma reflects the proportion of reduction in errors in predicting rankings on our dependent variable (skiing ability), given knowledge of the ranked distribution of the independent variable (family size). If the child's family size predicted skiing ability perfectly, gamma would be high; if not, gamma would be low.

Returning to the hypothesis: As we go up the family size scale, do the data indicate that there is a corresponding increase in the skiing-ability scale? In the data presented in Table 5.5, the gamma would be 0.93. This means that if we know a child's family size, it improves our ability to predict a child's ranking on skiing ability by 93 percent (compared with predicting skiing ability knowing nothing about a child's family size). Does this affirm the hypothesis? Yes. There is a positive association between family size and ability to ski (at least in this hypothetical example).

T A B L E 5.5   Skiing Ability by Family Size

Ability	Small Family	Mid-Sized Family	Large Family	Huge Family
Expert	0	0	5	30
Advanced	0	10	20	10
Intermediate	5	15	15	0
Beginner	35	15	0	0

Interval- and Ratio-Level Correlation   To do interval or ratio measurement, you need to be able to establish distances between the units of analysis. It is not good enough to have skiers arrayed in terms of expert, advanced, intermediate, and beginner. The amount of distance in ability between expert and advanced and the rest has to be specified. With ordinal measures such as skiing ability, the difference between expert and advanced may be quite unlike the difference between intermediate and beginner. With the specification of discrete distances in measurement comes the possibility of using a correlation statistic that employs units of distance (or size, etc.) to measure the association between variables.

Interval and ratio measurements specify a distance between units and allow the use of a formidable-sounding statistic by the name of Pearson's product-moment correlation coefficient, or **Pearson's *r*.**

To keep things simple, we developed a very elementary example: the relationship between the number of oil wells owned and the number of Hummers owned. Our sample consists of five oil well owners. To see what the mathematics of the Pearson's product-moment correlation accomplishes, consider two possible arrays of data. Suppose, first, that there is a correlation of +1.00 between number of oil wells and the number of Hummers. Figure 5.3 illustrates two sets of data for which that same correlation of +1.00 could be claimed.

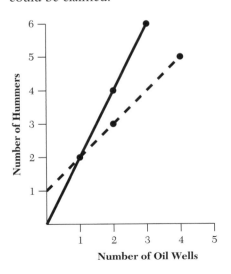

FIGURE 5.3   Relationship Between Number of Hummers and Number of Oil Wells

Notice the straight solid line that can be drawn connecting each case expressing the following relationship between the two variables: as the number of oil wells increases by 1, the number of Hummers increases by 2. A perfect correlation also results if the straight line should happen to fall at a different level. For example, the broken line shows that you can get a Hummer without an oil well. But for every extra Hummer, it appears necessary to sink a new well.

Now imagine an array of data in which the cases do not present themselves on a straight line. If the data were to appear as in Table 5.6 (these data are also plotted in Figure 5.4), no straight line can be drawn that connects all the cases. Imagine that there is one straight line that is closest to all the points on the chart—the line that minimizes the squared distance by which all the cases deviate from the line. Pearson's r, by a mathematical process, identifies how tightly the points cluster around an imaginary line that expresses the linear relationship.

For mathematical reasons (best left to mathematicians), the deviations of cases from the line are measured in terms of the squares of the distances $(a^2 + b^2 + c^2 + d^2)$ rather than simple distances $(a + b + c + d)$. The more distant the cases are from the best-fitting line, the lower the correlation of variable A with variable B. The Pearson's r for Figure 5.4 is +0.85.

The Pearson correlation statistic can be made to supply one other important piece of information. By squaring Pearson's r, we can find out what proportion of all the variation in the dependent variable is explained by variation in the independent variable. In the case of oil wells and Hummers in Figure 5.4, Pearson's r is +0.85, so $r^2 = 0.72 \times (0.85 \times 0.85)$. Thus, the number of oil wells

T A B L E   5.6   Number of Oil Wells and Hummers

Hummers	Oil Wells				
	One	Two	Three	Four	Five
One		1			
Two		1			
Three				1	
Four			1		
Five					1

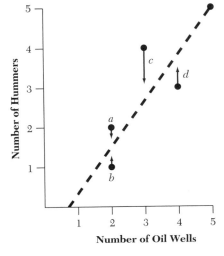

FIGURE 5.4 Best Fitting Line Describing Relationship Between Hummers and Oil Wells

a person has explains 72 percent of the number of Hummers owned. Other variables explain the remaining 28 percent of the variation.

Alternatively, if all of the points fall on the line (as in Figure 5.3) and r is +1.00, then r^2 would also be 1.00 (that is, $1 \times 1 = 1$)! The number of oil wells correlates perfectly with the number of Hummers, and there is no variation left over to be explained by the other factors. The study reported in Appendix B includes several scatter-plot figures similar to those in Figure 5.4 to illustrate graphically what various values of Pearson's r actually might look like.

As with each of the measures of association discussed here, Pearson's r tells us about correlation, which may or may not indicate a causal relationship. A significant r does not show that the number of oil wells causes people to own more Hummers, only that the two things go together. The actual relationship might be reversed (although, in this example, that might seem illogical).

We might find that two things are correlated yet have no clear-cut idea about which variable determines the other. Suppose a researcher finds that educational attainment is correlated with intelligence. Which causes which? Measures of association do not require that the researcher assume anything about causation.

Statistics do not establish causation; causation depends on the logic of relationships.

Notice what else this procedure does not accomplish. A Pearson's r of +1.00 indicates only that any variation in A is associated with a consistent variation in B. What it does not tell you is the number of units B varies in relation to A. It happens in the example in Figure 5.3 (solid line) that as the number of oil wells goes up by 1, the number of Hummers goes up by 2. But if the situation were such that for every increase of one oil well there was a consistent increase of one Hummer, or 1/2 of a Hummer, or 3 Hummers, a +1.00 result would still be obtained.

In mathematical terms, Pearson's r tells you only about the dispersion of cases around an imaginary straight line. It does not tell you the slope of the line or, in other words, the amount of change in B for every unit of variation in A. A separate statistical procedure involving advanced statistical concepts called regression analysis deals with this question.

Regression Analysis

The purpose of this general kind of measurement is to characterize the impact of variables on each other. **Regression analysis** adds a new level of sophistication to these characterizations. With regression, if you know the value of an independent variable, you can begin to predict the value of the dependent variable.

There are two basic forms of regression: bivariate regression and multiple regression. Bivariate regression, like correlation analysis, characterizes how changes in levels of a single independent variable are related to changes in a dependent variable. Multiple regression examines how several different independent variables are associated with a dependent variable.

As an example of bivariate regression, consider a simple example from major league baseball. Because professional baseball teams spend different amounts of money on player salaries, we might wonder whether higher levels of spending are associated with the number of games a team wins. How much of an effect does team payroll have on winning percentage? Bivariate regression helps to answer this question by summarizing the association between the two variables in terms of the following linear equation:

$$Y \text{ [winning percentage]} = a + bX \text{ [team payroll]}$$

Expressing the association in words, values of the Y variable (a team's winning percentage) are a function of some constant, plus some amount of the X variable. The question we are interested in is, does the amount a team spends on its players affect its success on the field? In other words, how much change in the Y variable (winning percentage) is associated with a one-unit change in the X variable (team payroll)? The answer lies in b, the regression coefficient.[16]

We can use data from the 2012 baseball season to test the hypothesis that teams with higher payrolls win more games.[17] For each of the 30 major league teams, we measured team payroll (the X variable) as the total a team spent on players, in millions of dollars. We measured winning percentage (the Y variable) as the percent of games the team won in 2012 at the half-way point of the season. Pearson's r correlation between the two variables is 0.30, illustrating that as teams spent more money, they won more games.

A bivariate regression shows that:

$$\text{Team winning percentage} =$$
$$44.7 \text{ percent} + 0.054 \times \text{team payroll (in \$ millions)}$$

This means that the **slope** of the relationship between a team's payroll and winning percentage was 0.054. Put differently, for each additional million dollars spent on player salaries by an average team, the team would win 0.054 percent more of its games. That might not sound like much, but the average team spent about \$98 million on player salaries for the 2012 season. Another \$100 million spent on talented players might have yielded 5.4 percent more victories (\$100 million $\times$ 0.054 = 5.4). Over the 162-game season, 5 more victories can be the difference between first and third place. These results show that a team spending the average amount on player salaries would win about 50 percent of its games (44.7 percent + (0.054 $\times$ \$98 million) = 49.99 percent, or a 0.499 record in baseball terms).[18]

Modeling winning percentage as being dependent on total team payroll explains just 10 percent of variation in winning percentage across the 30 major league teams. This means that other variables—injuries to star players, a skilled general manager, a strong pitching staff that was bought cheaply, young talent that is not paid very much, and other less tangible variables—may be more powerful in explaining why some teams win while others lose.[19] This example from baseball illustrates something we find sometimes in social science: Our regression models can leave a great deal unexplained because some of what we model may be the result of intangibles that are not easily quantified.

Consider another example. In Appendix B, Todd Donovan, David Denemark, and Shaun Bowler explore differences across nations in levels of public trust in government. As Table B.1 in Appendix B illustrates, less than 10 percent of survey respondents in Japan agreed that they could trust people in government "to do what is right" most of the time. In contrast, a majority of respondents in Denmark said they trusted their government when offered the same survey question. Americans appear much more trusting than Germans, Poles, and Japanese, but much less trusting than Danes, Finns, and Swiss. The research question here is straightforward: Why is trust so much higher in some nations than others?

Fortunately for these researchers, there is a large body of literature that offers explanations of cross-national variation in political trust. Some have proposed that trust or distrust of government is embedded in a nation's history and culture and that whatever the ill effects of high levels of distrust may be, nothing much can be done about it. Others claim that trust is greater where democratic institutions function better and that distrust is the product of short-term failures of government performance. The authors test some of these arguments by using correlation and bivariate regression. As one example, they examine the relationship between the percent of people in a nation who say they trust government (the dependent variable, or Y), and the percent of people who think that corruption is widespread in the public sector (the independent variable, or X).

The authors of the study found that, across 29 nations, the correlation between a nation's overall level of trust and a nation's overall perceptions of official corruption was −0.60. The slope of the relationship between these two variables is −0.36, with a Y-intercept of 39.0 and an r^2 of 0.35 (see Figure B.5 in Appendix B). The negative sign for the correlation coefficient indicates that in nations where there is more political corruption, there is less trust in government—a negative, or inverse, relationship. The slope of the relationship between corruption and trust estimated with regression analysis illustrates the linear relationship between

these two variables, that is, how much a one-unit change in the
independent variable (corruption, in this example) is associated
with change in the dependent variable (trust). In this case, the
−0.36 slope illustrates that for each 1 percent increase in the number of people in a country who think their public officials are
corrupt, there is a 0.36 percent decrease in the number who trust
government.

What about regression that involves more than one variable
(and what about an example that relates directly to politics)? As
an example of **multiple regression**, suppose you notice that
your friends differ widely in their level of involvement in electoral
politics. Activity might range across a spectrum, as illustrated here:

| nonvoter | voted in 5 of 10 recent elections | voted in all recent elections |

Why do some people vote more often than others? Factors
that occur prior to voting activism or independently of it would
include income levels, education levels, or levels of prior experience with politics (call them independent variables). Each could
logically be associated with the level of voting. Multiple regression
permits analysis of the effects of several independent variables at
the same time. This technique isolates the effect of a single independent variable while controlling for (or holding constant) the
effects of other independent variables.

To pursue the example, voter participation, the dependent
variable, could be operationalized in terms of a score derived
from the number of recent elections a person has voted in. The
more elections a person voted in, the higher the participation
score. For the sake of simplicity, we assume our measure of voter
participation ranges from 0 to 10.

As we have seen, measures of correlation make it possible to
see whether income and political participation, for example, are
positively or negatively related (whether participation goes up or
down as income rises). Correlation also establishes how closely
one varies in association with the other.

With knowledge of the correlation of income and participation, you can estimate whether a rich person is more or less likely
to be a more active voter than a poor person. If, however, you
would like to have a better chance of predicting the amount of

change in participation associated with each change in level of income, then regression analysis is required. To test for the effect of one independent variable on a dependent variable while controlling for the effects of one or more additional variables, multiple regression is required.

For example, we might expect that variation in voter participation is associated with both income and education. Multiple regression estimates statistically the unique effect of each variable on the dependent variable while holding other independent variables constant. Thus, we can see if education affects participation while controlling for income levels. Multiple regression tables typically report a series of b's (slopes, or regression coefficients) for each of the independent variables included in the analysis. These are interpreted as the amount of change in the dependent variable (Y) associated with a one-unit change in an independent variable (X_1), holding constant other included variables (X_2, X_3, and so on).

Recall the brief discussion about control and spuriousness from Chapter Four. Social scientists are often unable to use laboratories to control or hold constant the effects of multiple variables. It would be impossible as well as cruel, for example, to randomly distribute certain levels of income and education to different people, then place them under observation and wait to see whether participation occurs at different rates among people with different mixes of income and education. For this reason, social scientists often measure existing phenomena and then use statistical procedures such as multiple regression to control for the effects of variables that cannot (or should not) be manipulated.[20]

Interpreting multiple regression coefficients can become awkward when the independent variables are measured in different units. Because measures of income (dollars) range much more widely than measures of education (years of schooling), it is hard to compare regression coefficients for the two variables. But there is a statistical technique for making them comparable. The units can be expressed in terms of standard deviation units.

A normally distributed variable has about two-thirds of all observations fall somewhere within one **standard deviation** above or below the mean. Extreme scores lie two or three deviations above or below the mean.

A variable that has a lot of cases that are at the high and low ends of variation, regardless of how great the range of variation is, will have a large standard deviation. A variable for which the scores concentrate around the average will have a low standard deviation. This method of standardizing is used often in regression analysis.[21]

The resulting standardized regression coefficient is typically referred to as the **beta coefficient**; like Pearson's r, it usually varies from -1.00 to $+1.00$. In terms of the dependent variable in our example, voter participation, if we found that the beta coefficient for income was $+1.00$, this would indicate that a one standard-deviation-unit change in income is associated with a one standard-deviation-unit change in participation. If we found the beta to be $+0.50$, we would conclude that a one standard–deviation–unit change in income is associated with a half standard–deviation–unit change in participation.

The regression coefficient and the beta coefficient are one part of regression analysis. The other part is a multiple correlation statistic, $\boldsymbol{R}$ (not to be confused with Pearson's small r, which deals with a single independent variable). R reports the correlation between a group of independent variables and a dependent variable. In parallel fashion, there is $\boldsymbol{R^2}$, which indicates the proportion of the variation in the dependent variable explained by the group of independent variables under consideration.

Putting this all together, if we used a computer statistics package to conduct a multiple regression analysis of the effects that income and education had on political activism, our results would include b and beta for each independent variable as well as R^2, which describes the effects of all the independent variables. Because we have two independent variables in our example, we would have two unique b's, or slopes, and two unique betas. The b's are expressed in whatever units the dependent variable is measured in. So, if b for education is 0.25, every one-unit change in education is associated with a quarter-point increase in our voter participation score—with the effects of income held constant. If the beta for education is 0.10, a one standard–deviation–unit increase in education is associated with a .10 standard deviation increase in participation. If $R^2 = 0.56$, we would know that the two variables explain just over half of the variation in our participation measure.

As a way of summarizing what has been presented so far about measuring relationships between variables and to set the agenda for the remaining discussion, look at Table 5.7. Information in

TABLE 5.7   **Measures of Association, Correlation, and Regression**

Statistic[*]	Meaning
r	*Pearson's correlation coefficient:* the degree of covariance between two variables (−1.00 to +1.00)
r^2	*Coefficient of determination:* in bivariate regression, the proportion of the variation in a dependent variable explained by the changes in the independent variable (0 to +1.00)
R	*Multiple correlation statistic:* the degree of covariance in a dependent variable associated with changes in two or more independent variables (0 to +1.00)
R^2	*Coefficient of determination:* the proportion of the variation in a dependent variable explained by changes in two or more independent variables (0 to +1.00)
b	*Unstandardized regression coefficient: the amount of variation in a dependent variable that occurs with each unit of variation in the independent variable* (zero to infinity)
beta	*Standardized regression coefficient: the amount of variation in a dependent variable for each unit of variation in one or more independent variables where the units of all variables are made comparable in terms of standard deviations from the mean* (usually varies between −1.00 and +1.00)

[*]For purposes of this table, we are using Pearson's r as the only measure of correlation. For other measures, see footnote 2 in this chapter.

Table 5.7 can serve as a handy reference when you are reading articles in social science journals, as many of them publish results of regression analyses.

Why Multiple Regression? Control and Spuriousness

How do you establish the unique effect of one independent variable while the effects of others are held constant? Multiple regression analysis is the answer.

In Chapter Three we noted that scholars studying social capital were interested in how membership in voluntary groups is associated with political participation. In Appendix A, Robert Putnam provides evidence that low levels of group membership are associated with high levels of television viewing. He writes, "Even after controlling for education, income, age, race, place of residence, work status, and gender, TV viewing is strongly and negatively related to social trust and group membership."

Figure A.2 in Appendix A provides a visual illustration of how social scientists test if the unique effect of one variable on another—in this example the effect of television viewing on joining groups—holds when the effect of a third variable, education, is accounted for. In the example from Putnam, we can see that people who watch the least amount of TV join the most groups at every level of education. In other words, the negative relationship between watching TV and joining groups remains even after we control for the effect of education.

Putnam wants to isolate one variable as the prime suspect to explain the decline of social capital in America. In Appendix A, much of the evidence points to television viewing as the culprit. By controlling for many possible rival explanations, he can make a stronger claim that the deleterious effect of TV watching is not due to another factor that is not accounted for. This is the problem of spuriousness.

A result is said to be **spurious** if it can be explained away by another variable. A classic example of a spurious relationship is the high correlation between the number of fire trucks at the scene of the fire and the amount of damage caused by the fire. The conclusion seems simple: Additional trucks cause more damage! The omitted variable, of course, is the size of the fire. A bigger fire brings out more trucks and a bigger fire causes more damage.

To return to the question of social capital, what if people who frequently watched television simply had less time or energy to join social groups? It could be that many people now work longer hours or spend more time commuting. By the time they get home it may be too late to meet with any groups. This being so, they end up spending their evenings watching TV. From this perspective, TV viewing is not the main cause of the decline of social capital. Rather, it may be a variable that corresponds with another important variable (lack of free time) that causes people to forgo joining social groups.

One fundamental goal of any scientific endeavor is to control for other variables that might explain away an important result. In your own research, you might not use advanced statistics or laboratory experiments to control for any or all omitted variables that could explain away your observations. Nevertheless, you should consider how confident you are that your results are not spurious.

For Example

Spuriousness and Control—Sunscreen and Cancer

It is well known that excessive exposure to the sun's ultraviolet (UV) rays is correlated with increased incidence of skin cancer. The correlation is well established, and medical science has solid reason to make the claim of a causal relationship here: overexposure to UV rays causes skin cancers. As a result, the American Academy of Dermatology and the American Cancer Society recommend that people use sunscreen with a sun protection factor (SPF) of 15 or higher.

Establishing correlation and causation in medical research, however, as with much in the social sciences, can be difficult. Evidence comes in the form of asking many people about their behavior, tallying up their illnesses, and then running an analysis to see what is correlated with what. Scientists cannot readily expose people to various cancer-causing agents and then see what happens. As a result, evidence that sun exposure causes cancer, and that sunscreen works, is based far more on correlation than causation. There is greater certainty about the relationship between UV exposure and some forms of skin cancer (squamous cell) than other skin cancers (melanoma).

To complicate matters, some studies find a positive link between sunscreen and the incidence of cancer. More sunscreen, more skin cancer. Consider the multiple variables at play here: amount of UV exposure, amount of sunscreen used, and incidence of skin cancer. It may be that UV exposure is the main culprit, but that people who are in the sun longer also tend to use more sunscreen. If this is the case, a correlation between sunscreen use and skin cancer may be spurious.

SOURCE: Based on Judith Foreman, "Sunscreen Isn't Perfect, but Still Worth Using," *Boston Globe* (July 10, 2006); "Sunscreen Ingredient May Increase Skin Cancer Risk," *Science News* (May 7, 2012).

To take the discussion a few steps further, we can look at another example. Table 5.8 is taken from a study by Susan Welch, Michael Combs, and John Gruhl. They explore the question, do black judges make a difference? They examine the factors that affect trial judges' sentencing decisions. The authors wanted to know whether white judges treat criminal defendants differently than do black judges. The research question here is straightforward, do sentencing decisions depend upon a judge's race?

Previous research was inconclusive—different studies found contradictory results. The authors noticed that earlier researchers failed to control for such important independent variables as the severity of the defendant's crime, the defendant's previous record, and other characteristics of the judge (such as gender).

TABLE 5.8   **The Impact of a Judge's Race on Sentence Severity and the Decision to Incarcerate**

	Decision to Incarcerate		Sentence Severity		
	MLE	*MLE/SE*	*b*	*beta*	*t*
All Defendants					
No controls	0.10	2.10*	−0.48	−0.01	−0.67
Controls for defendant and crime	0.14	2.17*	−0.91	−0.02	−1.60
Controls for judge, defendant, and crime	0.11	1.67	−1.22	−0.03	−2.14*
White Defendants					
No controls	0.11	0.92	0.27	0.01	0.20
Controls for defendant and crime	0.35	2.19*	1.40	0.04	1.31
Controls for judge, defendant, and crime	0.35	2.18*	1.39	0.04	1.30
Black Defendants					
No controls	0.10	1.72	−0.80	−0.02	−0.96
Controls for defendant and crime	0.09	1.24	−1.59	−0.04	−2.40*
Controls for judge, defendant, and crime	0.06	0.78	−2.00	−0.05	−2.99*

CODING: Black judges = 1, white judges = 0. Controls for defendant and crime include the severity of the crime, whether the defendant pled guilty, the defendant's prior record, and whether or not he had a public defender. Additional controls for judicial characteristics include the judge's prosecutorial experience, sex, and years on the bench. N = 3,418 for all defendants, 763 for white defendants, and 2,655 for black defendants. *= significant at .05.

NOTE: MLE is the maximum likelihood estimate and SE is the standard error.

SOURCE: Susan Welch, Michael Combs, and John Gruhl, "Do Black Judges Make a Difference?" *American Journal of Political Science* 32, no. 1 (1988):126–136. Reproduced with permission of John Wiley & Sons, Inc.

Welch et al. develop their data from a sample of male defendants convicted of felonies between 1968 and 1979 in a large northeastern city. In one part of the analysis, they operationalize their dependent variable as the severity of the judge's sentence. They use a severity scale where 0 equals a suspended sentence; lower scores reflect fines and probation; higher scores reflect jail time; and the highest value, 93, equals life imprisonment. Because they wanted to control for multiple independent variables, they used multiple regression analysis.

Using a form of bivariate regression, they find that the judge's race (the independent variable) is not associated with sentence severity. That is, when they look only at the relationship between the judge's race and the severity of the sentence, there is no relationship.[22]

But when multiple regression is used, and they introduce controls for severity of the defendant's crime and other factors, they find a significant, albeit slight, difference.[23] Black judges are associated with a sentence that is 1.22 units lower on the severity scale of 0 to 93. This effect is particularly evident when the sample examined is limited to black defendants. Compared to white judges, black judges' sentences of black defendants are exactly two units lower in severity; however, there is more to the story.[24]

Probit and Logit Analysis

Welch and her colleagues also note that severity of sentencing is not the only aspect, or even the most critical aspect, of judicial sentencing decisions. Prior to deciding about the severity of the sentence, the judge must decide whether the defendant will or will not be incarcerated. Some people are let off with probation, and although convicted of a felony, they are not required to spend time in jail.

When the dependent variable is conceived in these terms, regression analysis cannot be applied. Correlation and regression analysis assume that the dependent variable is measured at the interval, or ordinal, level. Decision to incarcerate, however, is coded such that 1 = incarcerate and 0 = do not incarcerate. This being the case, we cannot talk about how a one-unit change in the independent variable produces a change of some number of units in the dependent variable.

Another form of analysis similar to multiple regression is designed to deal with these dichotomous (two-category) dependent variables.[25] Social science researchers often deal with dependent variables that are simple nominal categories such as "yes or no" answers to survey questions or how various factors affect a government's decision to adopt a public policy or fight in a war. **Probit and logit analysis** are being used with increasing frequency to address these questions.

Rather than producing regression coefficients or betas, probit produces a coefficient that is not easily interpretable on its own. With the aid of a mathematical formula (omitted here for simplicity's sake), these coefficients can be used to assess how changes in X affect the probability that Y will assume one value or another. This statistic can help answer the question as to whether a difference in the judge's race affects the probability that a felon will serve time in jail.[26]

Welch et al. use probit analysis to test the relationship between the independent variables and the decision to incarcerate.[27] They find that black judges are more likely to decide to incarcerate defendants than white judges. When the authors control for other variables, however, the significance of this effect disappears. It is important to note that the maximum likelihood estimates (MLEs) generated by logit and probit do not tell us much about the substantive impact of the independent variables. The logit results in Table 5.8 simply explain whether something has a statistically significant relationship with a judge's decision.

The probit analysis also shows that there are significant racial differences in the decision to incarcerate white defendants once controls for other factors are introduced into the analysis. White defendants are less likely to be sent to prison when sentenced by white judges; put differently, black judges are more likely to sentence white defendants to jail when severity of the crime and other factors are accounted for.

Welch and her colleagues conclude, after assessing all of the measures, that black judges do make a difference in the criminal justice system. Based on the results of the multiple regression and probit analyses of this particular sample, black judges appear slightly more likely than white judges (1) to sentence white defendants to prison and (2) to give slightly less severe sentences to black defendants. However, "in the decision about incarceration, black judges appear even-handed [as between black and white defendants], while white judges are less likely to send whites than blacks to jail."[28] Note that the authors qualify their results and make an effort to explain the multiple factors that might explain why blacks and whites behave in marginally different ways.

Although the nuances of race and sentencing may be subtle, these results can be used to challenge such gross generalizations as, "White (or black) judges are racists." We learn from modest results as much as from dramatic results.

As a way of summarizing what has been presented so far about measuring relationships between variables, see Table 5.9.

The central problem in regression has to do with sorting out the interrelated or statistically overlapping effects of several independent variables on the dependent variable. The problem can be

TABLE 5.9 **Measurements of Relations Between Variables**

Correlation	The *degree* of association or covariation between two interval- or ratio-level variables. Direction of the relationship is indicated by the plus or minus sign.
Bivariate Regression	The *amount* of change in an interval- or ratio-level dependent variable associated with a one-unit change in a *single* independent variable.
Multiple Regression	The *amount* of change in an interval- or ratio-level dependent variable explained by *several* variables. Tests for the unique effect of each independent variable. Used in conjunction with R^2, which reports the proportion of variation in the dependent variable explained by the independent variables acting together.
Probit and Logit Analysis	A form of multiple regression wherein the dependent variable is *dichotomous* (e.g., yes/no, for/against). Examines how a unit change in an independent variable will produce a change in the *probability* that the dependent variable will take one value or the other.

attacked, though rarely resolved completely, by precise operationalization, by analysis of the covariance of similar independent variables, and by such techniques as probit analysis.

In any multiple regression model or probit analysis, a good many technicalities, precautions, and limiting assumptions need to be considered before the results are taken seriously. The logic of the analysis, however, is what we are after here. Several variables affect judicial decisions. The researchers' logic suggests that some of these variables need to be accounted for or controlled for statistically in order that they might make conclusions about a variable they are particularly interested in: namely, race. In the example, it appears that there are some mildly significant effects of race, even after we control for other factors such as severity of the crime.

As technical as the statistics make it seem, regression and probit analysis, like science in general, begin with creativity and imagination. The first part of regression analysis involves figuring out which variables to test for—and this comes from an awareness of theory and a keen sense of the subject under investigation. The usefulness of regression analysis is that it indicates the possibilities for even more precise measurement of relations between variables in hypotheses.

COMPUTERS AND STATISTICS

The development of statistical software for computers makes it possible for researchers to process data quickly and efficiently. A certain amount of mathematical and conceptual background used to be the prerequisite for the calculation of statistics. Now computers can do the mathematics. In some instances, this means that data are manipulated in ways that are not appropriate to the level of measurement.

Although it is possible to leave the mathematics to a computer, it is dangerous to use statistical techniques without being fully aware of the conceptual foundations for mathematical processes. Just because a software package can produce a correlation statistic for two variables does not mean that the measurement standards necessary for correlation have been met. It is tempting to resort to software-produced statistics that seem to offer great precision; however, there is no substitute for a careful assessment of the properties and characteristics of the data according to the guidelines suggested here (see Figure 5.1).

Statistics do not create data; they describe it. Just as it would be nonsensical to describe something abstract by referring to its color or other physical properties, so is it misleading to claim statistical relationships where none can be calculated.

The refinements we discussed are themselves just the beginnings of what can be done to elaborate and improve research strategies. We sought only to map the major pathways of understanding and technique. Further development of research skills usually comes not so much from forced marches through methodology texts as from the motivation generated by an interesting project. As the project develops, methodological matters become more significant and more rewarding to learn.

In pursuing methodological understanding, however, beware of a simple "cookbook" approach. Understand the idea of what you are doing before enlisting the specific techniques by which it can be accomplished. That, at least, is the bias of this book and the experience of its authors. The wealth of detail found in the technical literature on methodology becomes much more digestible if the relatively simple ideas that underlie the calculations can be seen. Ideas provide frameworks for the mechanics of technique.

CONCLUSIONS

This little book provides a sketch of the scientific method as applied to the study of social and political questions. In closing, it is important to reiterate that social science does not function the same as natural science. The concepts we deal with are often less well defined, less agreed upon, or both. With broad, interesting social questions, the application of a scientific method may be particularly challenging. Consider these questions: Who has power? How is power used? What is the nature of happiness? Why are some people happier than others? What is wealth? Why are some people wealthier than others? Answering these requires that we define and measure complex phenomena. One person's definition of something like happiness, or power, may be quite different than another person's. Moreover, it can be difficult to be engaged in social science without some measure of subjectivity. Our values affect what things like power, happiness, and wealth actually are.

This stands in contrast to one of the great promises of science: objectivity. The scientific method offers a rigorous process to help researchers find answers that are not overly affected by the influence of personal prejudice and bias. Ideally, hypotheses are judged by the statistical significance of test results rather than by the researcher's personal values.

Although the scientific method provides rigor, in reality, a great deal of social science is subjective. People are drawn to subjects they are interested in. Decisions about how we define and measure things are affected by our personal understanding of the world. This is not to say that the scientific method cannot be applied to questions about the social world, but social science requires creativity. Advances in our understanding of the world occur when people imagine new questions and new ways of answering them.

CONCEPTS INTRODUCED

Measurement
Properties of
    variables
Nominal

Ordinal
Interval
True zero
Ratio scale

Arbitrary zero
Probability
Level of
    significance

Probability sample	Direction of	Multiple regression
Stratification	association	Standard deviation
Random sampling	scale of correlation	Beta coefficient
Sample bias	Contingency	R
Association	coefficient	R^2
Descriptive	Pearson's r	Spurious
statistics	Regression analysis	Probit and logit
Correlation	Slope	analysis

QUESTIONS FOR DISCUSSION

1. Recall that samples are used to estimate something about a larger population. Considering this, how might the sampling technique and method used to gather the Perot data cause the results to be biased?

2. Examine the questions in Table 5.1 taken from the Perot survey. How might the wording of the questions introduce errors in measuring the attitudes of respondents?

3. Can you think of better ways to word the survey questions listed in Table 5.2?

4. Is a baseball team's winning percentage an interval or ordinal variable? What about the place the team finishes in its division (first, last, and so on)? Which is a more valid measure of a team's performance? Consider that the St. Louis Cardinals won the 2006 World Series, but their 0.516 (51.6 percent) winning percentage during the regular season was only thirteenth best in the major leagues.

5. Look at Figure B.1 in Appendix B. What might the scatterplot look like if the Pearson's correlation (r) statistic was actually 1.0? What might it look like if the correlation (r) was only 0.25?

ENDNOTES

1. This begs the question of what is nationality? In this case, we mean the country someone is a citizen of. It could also be classified based of nation of origin, or other factors.

2. From Sidney Siegel, *Nonparametric Statistics for the Social Sciences* (New York: McGraw-Hill, 1956), p. 30. See also Chava Frankfort-Nachmias and David

Nachmias, *Research Methods in the Social Sciences*, 6th ed. (New York: St. Martin's, 2000), Chapter 7.

For those who are familiar with statistics, the following is a *partial* list of examples of statistics appropriate for each level:

Nominal: mode, frequency, contingency table

Ordinal: median, percentile, Spearman's rho, Kendall's tau, Goodman–Kruskal's gamma

Interval: mean, standard deviation, Pearson's product moment correlation, multiple correlation

Ratio: geometric mean, coefficient of variation, ordinary least squares regression

3. An influential critique of positivism from within the philosophy of science can be found in W. V. O. Quine, "The Two Dogmas of Empiricism," *From a Logical Point of View*, ed. W. V. O. Quine (New York: Harper & Row, 1961). See also Alexander Rosenberg, *The Structure of Biological Science* (Cambridge, U.K.: Cambridge University Press, 1985).

4. For a lucid and accessible discussion of significance testing, see Lawrence Mohr, *Understanding Significance Tests*, Sage University Paper Series on Quantitative Applications in the Social Sciences, no. 73 (Beverly Hills, Calif.: Sage Publications, 1990).

5. We thank Albert Klumpp for this example.

6. See Pew Research Center. "Cell Phones and Election Polls: An Update." October 13, 2010.

7. After the U.S. Supreme Court intervened to stop recounting, the final official count showed that George W. Bush won Florida by 537 votes out of 5.963 million—or 48.85 percent. Under this count, Gore received 48.84 percent. Florida's result gave Bush a majority of Electoral College votes.

8. Exit polls tend to use large, stratified, state-specific samples, which lowers the margin of error from the standard ± 3 percent used in major media polls.

9. Postelection review of uncounted punch cards, "hanging chads," "caterpillar ballots," "butterfly ballots," and illegally counted overseas ballots demonstrate that several thousand more people attempted to vote for Gore than for Bush in the Florida election. See Jonathan Wand et al., "The Butterfly Did It: The Aberrant Vote for Buchanan in Palm Beach County, Florida," *American Political Science Review*, 95, no. 4 (2001): pp. 793–810; David Barstow and Don Van Natta Jr., "How Bush Stole Florida: Mining the Overseas Absentee Ballots," *New York Times* (July 15, 2001); Kosuke Imai and Gary King, "Did Illegally Counted Overseas Ballots Decide the 2000 U.S. Presidential Election?" Manuscript (Department of Government, Harvard University, 2001).

10. The 1936 election made George Gallup famous. He used a much smaller and relatively random "quota" sample to predict that Roosevelt would win. For an account of polling in this election, see David W. Moore, *The Superpollsters* (New York: Four Walls Eight Windows, 1992). Gallup's 1936 quota method caused another famous failure, however, when his sample led him to predict that Dewey would defeat Truman in 1948. Since 1948, Gallup and other pollsters have come to use probability samples.

11. Daniel Goleman, "Pollsters Enlist Psychologists in Quest for Unbiased Results," *New York Times* (September 7, 1993), pp. B5, B8. Also see *The Public Perspective* (Roper Center for Public Research, May/June 1993).

12. An accessible introduction to public opinion polling is Herbert Asher, *Polling and the Public: What Every Citizen Should Know* (Washington, D.C.: CQ Press, 2004).

13. The chi-square value for the data in Table 3.3 is very high, as is the sample size (20,716). This means that there is a very low probability that group memberships are *independent* of age cohort.

14. See G. W. Bohrnstedt and D. Knoke, *Statistics for Social Data Analysis* (Itasca, Ill.: F. E. Peacock, 1988), p. 310.

15. Other chi-square–based statistics that assess association among variables measured at this level on a scale of 0 to 1 are Cramer's v and phi.

16. In algebraic terms, b represents the slope of the relationship between X and Y. Mixing algebra with baseball, b would be the "rise over the run" if we were to plot the relationship between Y and X on a graph.

17. Data for winning percentages were measured as of July 5, 2012. Payroll data were drawn from *USA Today* 2012 MLB Salaries Database. Baseball writers maintain a curious tradition of reporting a team's record in terms of "percentages" when, in fact, they actually represent proportions. That is, a team is winning when the percentage is greater than .500. Our data are recorded as true percentages, so a winning record would be something greater than 50.0 percent. If we entered proportions into our analysis rather than percentages, b would be expressed in units that would be 100 times smaller.

18. The *constant* to the intercept of the Y axis (44.7 percent) represents what the value of Y would be if X were zero (0)—in this example the percent of games an unpaid team of talented amateurs would be able to win in a season.

19. Because Pearson's r for this example was 0.32, we know that spending explains 10 percent of variation in team winning percentages ($0.32 \times 0.32 = 0.10$). One reason that the *model fit* represented by r^2 is just 0.10 is that a number of teams with below-average payrolls had better records at the midpoint of the 2012 season (the Pittsburgh Pirates and the Washington Nationals), while other teams (the Philadelphia Phillies and Boston Red Sox) spent more than all but one other team, but they lost most of their games.

20. A treatment of the mathematics of regression is beyond the scope of this book, but countless texts are available on the topic. Brief, accessible introductions can be found in L. Schroeder, D. Sjoquist, and P. Stephan, *Understanding Regression Analysis*, Sage University Paper Series on Quantitative Applications in the Social Sciences, no. 57 (Beverly Hills, Calif.: Sage Publications, 1986), or M. Lewis-Beck, *Applied Regression,* Sage University Paper Series on Quantitative Applications in the Social Sciences, no. 22 (Beverly Hills, Calif.: Sage Publications, 1980).

21. A number of technical problems are associated with using standardized regression coefficients. Some scholars suggest that findings should simply be expressed in terms of "real" units. See Gary King, "How Not to Lie with Statistics," *American Journal of Political Science* 30, no. 3 (1986): 666–687.

22. Beta = −0.01, *b* = −0.48; not significant.

23. Beta = −0.03, *b* = −1.22.

24. Beta = −0.05, *b* = −2.00.

25. The procedure is referred to as probit or logit analysis, or "logistic regression" in some cases. Probit and logit differ slightly in the assumptions made about the underlying distribution of the dependent variable. See J. Aldrich and F. Nelson, *Linear Probability, Logit and Probit Models*, Sage University Paper Series on Quantitative Applications in the Social Sciences, no. 45 (Beverly Hills, Calif.: Sage Publications, 1984).

26. When correlation and regression are used to test for a relationship, the statistics test how well the data are represented by a straight line or slope. When probit analysis is used, the statistic tests how well the relationship between X and Y is represented by an S-shaped curve. A statistic that searches for a linear association (correlation and regression) between the decision to incarcerate (Y) and the severity of the crime (X) might miss the relationship and lead to many errors in prediction.

27. In Welch et al., "Do Black Judges Make a Difference?," Table 1, the probit coefficients are referred to as MLEs (maximum likelihood estimates). Welch et al. deem the coefficient significant if it is at least twice the size of its standard error (MLE/SE > 2.0).

28. Welch et al., p. 134.

Appendix A

Tuning In, Tuning Out: The Strange Disappearance of Social Capital in America

ROBERT D.PUTNAM
Harvard University

For the last year or so, I have been wrestling with a difficult mystery. It is, if I am right, a puzzle of some importance to the future of American democracy. It is a classic brain-teaser, with a corpus delicti, a crime scene strewn with clues, and many potential suspects. As in all good detective stories, however, some plausible miscreants turn out to have impeccable alibis, and some important clues hint at portentous developments that occurred long before the curtain rose. Moreover, like Agatha Christie's *Murder on the Orient Express*, this crime may have had more than one perpetrator, so that we shall need to sort out ringleaders from

SOURCE: From "Tuning In, Tuning Out: The Strange Disappearance of Social Capital in the United States," the 1995 Ithiel de Sola Pool Lecture, PS: Political Science and Politics, 28(4), pp. 664–683.

accomplices. Finally, I need to make clear at the outset that I am not yet sure that I have solved the mystery. In that sense, this represents work-in-progress. I have a prime suspect that I am prepared to indict, but the evidence is not yet strong enough to convict, so I invite your help in sifting clues.

THEORIES AND MEASURES OF SOCIAL CAPITAL

Several years ago I conducted research on the arcane topic of local government in Italy (Putnam 1993). That study concluded that the performance of government and other social institutions is powerfully influenced by citizen engagement in community affairs, or what (following Coleman 1990) I termed social capital. I am now seeking to apply that set of ideas and insights to the urgent problems of contemporary American public life.

By social capital, I mean features of social life—networks, norms, and trust—that enable participants to act together more effectively to pursue shared objectives. Whether or not their shared goals are praiseworthy is, of course, entirely another matter. To the extent that the norms, networks, and trust link substantial sectors of the community and span underlying social cleavages—to the extent that the social capital is of a "bridging" sort—then the enhanced cooperation is likely to serve broader interests and to be widely welcomed.…

Social capital, in short, refers to social connections and the attendant norms and trust. Who benefits from these connections, norms, and trust—the individual, the wider community, or some faction within the community—must be determined empirically, not definitionally.[1] … For present purposes, I am concerned with forms of social capital that, generally speaking, serve civic ends.

Social capital in this sense is closely related to political participation in the conventional sense, but these terms are not synonymous. Political participation refers to our relations with political institutions. Social capital refers to our relations with one another. Sending a check to a PAC is an act of political participation, but it does not embody or create social capital. Bowling in a league or having coffee with a friend embodies and creates social capital, though these are not acts of political participation. (A grassroots political movement or a traditional urban machine is a social capital-intensive form of political participation.) I use the term "civic engagement" to refer to people's connections with the life of their communities, not merely with politics. Civic engagement is correlated with political participation in a narrower sense, but whether they move in lock step is an empirical question, not a logical certitude. Some forms of individualized political participation, such as check-writing, for example, might be rising at the same time that social connectedness was on the wane. Similarly, although social trust—trust in other people—and political trust—trust in political authorities—might be empirically related, they are logically quite distinct. I might well trust my neighbors without trusting city hall, or vice versa.

The theory of social capital presumes that, generally speaking, the more we connect with other people, the more we trust them, and vice versa. At least in the contexts I have so far explored, this presumption generally turns out to be true: social trust and civic engagement are strongly correlated. That is, with or without controls for education, age, income, race, gender, and so on, people who join are people who trust.[2] Moreover, this is true across different countries, and across different states in the United States, as well as across individuals, and it is true of all sorts of groups.[3] Sorting out which way causation flows—whether joining causes trusting or trusting causes joining—is complicated both theoretically and methodologically, although John Brehm and Wendy Rahn (1995) report evidence that the causation flows mainly from joining to trusting. Be that as it may, civic connections and social trust move together. Which way are they moving?

BOWLING ALONE: TRENDS IN CIVIC ENGAGEMENT

Evidence from a number of independent sources strongly suggests that America's stock of social capital has been shrinking for more than a quarter century.

- Membership records of such diverse organizations as the PTA, the Elks club, the League of Women Voters, the Red Cross, labor unions, and even bowling leagues show that participation in many conventional voluntary associations has declined by roughly 25–50 percent over the last two to three decades (Putnam 1995, 1996).

- Surveys of the time budgets of average Americans in 1965, 1975, and 1985, in which national samples of men and women recorded every single activity undertaken during the course of a day, imply that the time we spend on informal socializing and visiting is down (perhaps by one quarter) since 1965, and that the time we devote to clubs and organizations is down even more sharply (probably by roughly half) over this period.

- While Americans' interest in politics has been stable or even growing over the last three decades, and some forms of participation that require moving a pen, such as signing petitions and writing checks, have increased significantly, many measures of collective participation have fallen sharply (Rosenstone and Hansen 1993; Putnam 1996), including attending a rally or speech (off 36 percent between 1973 and 1993), attending a meeting on town or school affairs (off 39 percent), or working for a political party (off 56 percent).

- Evidence from the General Social Survey demonstrates, at all levels of education and among both men and women, a drop of roughly one quarter in group membership since 1974 and a drop of roughly one third in social trust since 1972.[4] ... Slumping membership has afflicted all sorts of groups, from sports clubs and professional associations to literary discussion groups and labor unions.[5] ... Furthermore, Gallup polls report that church attendance fell by roughly 15 percent during the 1960s and has remained at that lower level ever since, while data from the National Opinion Research Center suggest that the decline continued during the 1970s and 1980s and by now amounts to roughly 30 percent (Putnam 1996).
  ...

A fuller audit of American social capital would need to account for apparent counter-trends. Some observers believe, for example, that support groups and neighborhood watch groups are proliferating, and few deny that the last several decades have witnessed explosive growth in interest groups represented in Washington.... However, these are not really associations in which members meet one another. Their members' ties are to common symbols and ideologies, but not to each other.... With due regard to various kinds of counter-evidence, I believe that the weight of the available evidence confirms that Americans today are significantly less engaged with their communities than was true a generation ago.

Of course, lots of civic activity is still visible in our communities. American civil society is not moribund. Indeed, evidence suggests that America still outranks many other countries in the degree of our community involvement and social trust (Putnam 1996). But if we compare ourselves, not with other countries but with our parents, the best available evidence suggests that we are less connected with one another.

This prologue poses a number of important questions that merit further debate:

- Is it true that America's stock of social capital has diminished?

- Does it matter?

- What can we do about it?

The answer to the first two questions is, I believe, "yes," but I cannot address them further in this setting. Answering the third question—which ultimately concerns me most—depends, at least in part, on first understanding the causes of the strange malady afflicting American civic life. This is the mystery I seek to unravel here: Why, beginning in the 1960s and accelerating in the 1970s and 1980s, did the fabric of American community life begin to fray? Why are more Americans bowling alone?

EXPLAINING THE EROSION OF SOCIAL CAPITAL

Many possible answers have been suggested for this puzzle:

- Busyness and time pressure

- Economic hard times (or, according to alternative theories, material affluence)

- Residential mobility

- Suburbanization

- The movement of women into the paid labor force and the stresses of two-career families

- Disruption of marriage and family ties

- Changes in the structure of the American economy, such as the rise of chain stores, branch firms, and the service sector
- The sixties (most of which actually happened in the seventies), including
  ◇ Vietnam, Watergate, and disillusion with public life
  ◇ The cultural revolt against authority (sex, drugs, and so on)
- Growth of the welfare state
- The civil rights revolution
- Television, the electronic revolution, and other technological changes

Most respectable mystery writers would hesitate to tally up this many plausible suspects, no matter how energetic the fictional detective. I am not yet in a position to address all these theories—certainly not in any definitive form—but we must begin to winnow the list. To be sure, a social trend as pervasive as the one we are investigating probably has multiple causes, so our task is to assess the relative importance of such factors as these.

A solution, even a partial one, to our mystery must pass several tests.

Is the proposed explanatory factor correlated with trust and civic engagement? If not, it is difficult to see why that factor should even be placed in the lineup. For example, many women have entered the paid labor force during the period in question, but if working women turned out to be more engaged in community life than housewives, it would be harder to attribute the downturn in community organizations to the rise of two-career families.

Is the correlation spurious? If parents, for example, were more likely to be joiners than childless people, that might be an important clue. However, if the correlation between parental status and civic engagement turned out to be entirely spurious, due to the effects of (say) age, we would have to remove the declining birth rate from our list of suspects.

Is the proposed explanatory factor changing in the relevant way? Suppose, for instance, that people who often move have shallower community roots. That could be an important part of the answer to our mystery only if residential mobility itself had risen during this period.

Is the proposed explanatory factor vulnerable to the claim that it might be the result of civic disengagement, not the cause? For example, even if newspaper readership were closely correlated with civic engagement across individuals and across time, we would need to weigh the possibility that reduced newspaper circulation is the result (not the cause) of disengagement.

Against that set of benchmarks, let us consider various potential influences on social capital formation.

EDUCATION

Human capital and social capital are closely related, for education has a very powerful effect on trust and associational membership, as well as many other forms of social and political participation. Education is by far the strongest correlate that I have discovered of civic engagement in all its forms, including social trust and membership in many different types of groups.[6] ... Education, in short, is an extremely powerful predictor of civic engagement....

Education is in part a proxy for social class and economic differences, but when income, social status, and education are used together to predict trust and group membership, education continues to be the primary influence.... In short, highly educated people are much more likely to be joiners and trusters, partly because they are better off economically, but mostly because of the skills, resources, and inclinations that were imparted to them at home and in school.

It is widely recognized that Americans today are better educated than our parents and grandparents. It is less often appreciated how massively and rapidly this trend has transformed the educational composition of the adult population during just the last two decades. Since 1972, the proportion of all adults with ... more than 12 years has nearly doubled, rising from 28 percent to 50 percent....

Thus, education boosts civic engagement sharply, and educational levels have risen massively. Unfortunately, these two undeniable facts only deepen our central mystery. By itself, the rise in educational levels should have increased social capital during the last 20 years.... By contrast, however, the actual GSS figures show a net decline since the early 1970s....

Thus, this first investigative foray leaves us more mystified than before. We may nevertheless draw two useful conclusions from these findings, one methodological and one substantive:

1. Since education has such a powerful effect on civic engagement and social trust, we need to take account of educational differences in our exploration of other possible factors, in order to be sure that we do not confuse the consequences of education with the possible effects of other variables.

2. Whatever forces lie behind the slump in civic engagement and social trust, those forces have affected all levels in American society. The mysterious disengagement of the last quarter century seems to have afflicted all echelons of our society.

PRESSURES OF TIME AND MONEY

Americans certainly feel busier now than a generation ago: the proportion of us who report feeling "always rushed" jumped by half between the mid-1960s and the mid-1990s (Robinson and Godbey 1995). Probably the most obvious suspect behind our tendency to drop out of community affairs is pervasive busyness. And lurking nearby in the shadows are those endemic economic pressures so much discussed nowadays—job insecurity and declining real wages, especially among the lower two thirds of the income distribution.

Yet, however culpable busyness and economic insecurity may appear at first glance, it is hard to find any incriminating evidence. In fact, the balance of the evidence argues that pressures of time and money are apparently not important contributors to the puzzle we seek to solve.

In the first place, time budget studies do not confirm the thesis that Americans are, on average, working longer than a generation ago. On the contrary, Robinson and Godbey (1995) report a five-hour per week gain in free time for the average American between 1965 and 1985, due partly to reduced time spent on housework and partly to earlier retirement. Their claim Americans have more leisure time now than several decades ago is, to be sure, contested by other observers. Schor (1991), for example, reports evidence that our work hours are lengthening, especially for women. Whatever the resolution of that controversy, however, the thesis that attributes civic disengagement to longer workdays is rendered much less plausible by looking at the correlation between work hours, on the one hand, and social trust and group membership, on the other.

The available evidence strongly suggests that, in fact, long hours on the job are not associated with lessened involvement in civic life or reduced social trust. Quite the reverse: Results from the General Social Survey show that employed people belong to somewhat more groups than those outside the paid labor force. Even more striking is the fact that among workers, longer hours are linked to more civic engagement, not less.[7] This surprising discovery is fully consistent with evidence from the time budget studies. Robinson (1990a) reports that, unsurprisingly, people who spend more time at work do feel more rushed, and these harried souls do spend less time eating, sleeping, reading books, engaging in hobbies, and just doing nothing. Compared to the rest of the population, they also spend a lot less time watching television—almost 30 percent less. However, they do not spend less time on organizational activity....

... Moreover, the nationwide falloff in joining and trusting is perfectly mirrored among full-time workers, among part-time workers, and among those outside the paid labor force. So if people are dropping out of community life, long hours do not seem to be the reason.

If time pressure is not the culprit we seek, how about financial pressures? ... The declines in engagement and trust are actually somewhat greater among the more affluent segments of the American public than among the poor and middle-income wage-earners.... In short, neither objective nor subjective economic well-being has inoculated Americans against the virus of civic disengagement; if anything, affluence has slightly exacerbated the problem....

MOBILITY AND SUBURBANIZATION

Many studies have found that residential stability and such related phenomena as homeownership are associated with greater civic engagement. At an earlier stage in this investigation (Putnam 1995, 30), I observed that "mobility, like frequent repotting of plants, tends to disrupt root systems, and it takes time for an up-rooted individual to put down new roots." I must now report, however, that further inquiry fully exonerates residential mobility from any responsibility for our fading civic engagement. Data from the U.S. Bureau of the Census 1995 (and earlier years) show that rates of residential mobility have been remarkably constant over the last half century. In fact, to the extent that there has been any change at all, both long-distance and short-distance mobility have declined over the last five decades. During the 1950s, 20 percent of Americans changed residence each year and 6.9 percent annually moved across county borders; during the 1990s, the comparable figures are 17 percent and 6.6 percent. Americans, in short, are today slightly more rooted residentially than a generation ago. If the verdict on the economic distress interpretation had to be nuanced, the verdict on mobility is unequivocal. This theory is simply wrong.

But if moving itself has not eroded our social capital, what about the possibility that we have moved to places—especially the suburbs—that are less congenial to social connectedness? To test this theory, we must first examine the correlation between place of residence and social capital. In fact, social connectedness does differ by community type, but the differences turn out to be modest and in directions that are inconsistent with the theory....

THE CHANGING ROLE OF WOMEN

Most of (my generation's) mothers were housewives, and most of them invested heavily in social capital formation—a jargony way of referring to untold, unpaid hours in church suppers, PTA meetings, neighborhood coffee klatches, and visits to friends and relatives. The movement of women out of the home and into the paid labor force is probably the most portentous social change of the last half-century. However welcome and overdue the feminist revolution may be, it is hard to believe that it has had no impact on social connectedness. Could this be the primary reason for the decline of social capital over the last generation?

Some patterns in the available survey evidence seem to support this claim. All things considered, women belong to somewhat fewer voluntary associations than men (Edwards, Edwards, and

Watts 1984). On the other hand, time budget studies suggest that women spend more time on those groups and more time in informal social connecting than men (Robinson and Godbey 1995). Although the absolute declines in joining and trusting are approximately equivalent among men and women, the relative declines are somewhat greater among women. Controlling for education, memberships among men have declined at a rate of about 10–15 percent a decade, compared to about 20–25 percent a decade for women....

As we saw earlier, however, work status itself seems to have little net impact on group membership or on trust. Housewives belong to different types of groups than do working women (more PTAs, for example, and fewer professional associations), but in the aggregate working women are actually members of slightly more voluntary associations.[8] Moreover, the overall declines in civic engagement are somewhat greater among housewives than among employed women. Comparison of time budget data between 1965 and 1985 (Robinson and Godbey 1995) seems to show that employed women as a group are actually spending more time on organizations than before, while nonemployed women are spending less. This same study suggests that the major decline in informal socializing since 1965 has also been concentrated among nonemployed women.

The central fact, of course, is that the overall trends are down for all categories of women (and for men, too—even bachelors), but the figures suggest that women who work full-time actually may have been more resistant to the slump than those who do not.

Thus, although women appear to have borne a disproportionate share of the decline in civic engagement over the last two decades, it is not easy to find any micro-level data that tie that fact directly to their entry into the labor force. It is hard to control for selection bias in these data, of course, because women who have chosen to enter the workforce doubtless differ in many respects from women who have chosen to stay home. Perhaps one reason that community involvement appears to be rising among working women and declining among working housewives is that precisely the sort of women who, in an earlier era, were most involved with their communities have been disproportionately likely to enter the workforce, thus simultaneously lowering the average level of civic engagement among the remaining homemakers and raising the average among women in the workplace. Obviously, we have not been running a great national controlled experiment on the effects of work on women's civic engagement, and in any event the patterns in the data are not entirely clear. Contrary to my own earlier speculations, however, I can find little evidence to support the hypothesis that the movement of women into the workplace over the last generation has played a major role in the reduction of social connectedness and civic engagement. On the other hand, I have no clear alternative explanation for the fact that the relative declines are greater among women than men. Since this evidence is at best circumstantial, perhaps the best interim judgment here is the famous Scots verdict: not proven.

MARRIAGE AND FAMILY

Another widely discussed social trend that more or less coincides with the downturn in civic engagement is the breakdown of the traditional family unit—mom, dad, and the kids. Since the family itself is, by some accounts, a key form of social capital, perhaps its eclipse is part of the explanation for the reduction in joining and trusting in the wider community. What does the evidence show?

First of all, evidence of the loosening of family bonds is unequivocal. In addition to the century-long increase in divorce rates (which accelerated in the mid-1960s to the mid-1970s and then leveled off), and the more recent increase in single-parent families, the incidence of one-person households has more than doubled since 1950, in part because of the rising number of widows living alone (Caplow, Bahr, Modell, and Chadwick 1991, 47, 106, 113). The net effect of all these changes, as reflected in the General Social Survey, is that the proportion of all American adults who are currently unmarried climbed from 28 percent in 1974 to 48 percent in 1994.

Second, married men and women do rank somewhat higher on both our measures of social capital. That is, controlling for education, age, race, and so on, single people—both men and women, divorced, separated, and never-married—are significantly less trusting and less engaged civically than married people.[9] Roughly speaking, married men and women are about a third more trusting and belong to about 15–25 percent more groups than comparable single men and women. (Widows and widowers are more like married people than single people in this comparison.)

In short, successful marriage (especially if the family unit includes children) is statistically associated with greater social trust
and civic engagement. Thus, some part of the decline in both trust
and membership is tied to the decline in marriage....

My own verdict (based in part on additional evidence to be
introduced later) is that the disintegration of marriage is probably
an accessory to the crime, but not the major villain of the piece.

THE RISE OF THE WELFARE STATE

Circumstantial evidence, particularly the timing of the downturn
in social connectedness, has suggested to some observers (for
example, Fukuyama 1995, 313–314) that an important cause—
perhaps even the cause—of civic disengagement is big government
and the growth of the welfare state. By "crowding out" private
initiative, it is argued, state intervention has subverted civil society.
This is a much larger topic than I can address in detail here, but a
word or two may be appropriate.

On the one hand, some government policies have almost
certainly had the effect of destroying social capital. For example, the
so-called slum clearance policies of the 1950s and 1960s replaced
physical capital by disrupting existing community ties. It is also con-
ceivable that certain social expenditures and tax policies may have
created disincentives for civic-minded philanthropy. On the other
hand, it is much harder to see which government policies might be
responsible for the decline in bowling leagues and literary clubs.

One empirical approach to this issue is to examine differences
in civic engagement and public policy across different political jur-
isdictions to see whether swollen government leads to shriveled
social capital. Among the U.S. states, however, differences in social
capital appear essentially uncorrelated with various measures of
welfare spending or government size.[10]...

RACE AND THE CIVIL RIGHTS
REVOLUTION

Race is such an absolutely fundamental feature of American social
history that nearly every other feature of our society is connected
to it in some way. Thus, it seems intuitively plausible that race

might somehow have played a role in the erosion of social capital over the last generation. In fact, some observers (both black and white) have noted that the decline in social connectedness and social trust began just after the greatest successes of the civil rights revolution of the 1960s. To some, that coincidence has suggested the possibility of a kind of sociological "white flight," as legal desegregation of civic life led whites to withdraw from community associations.

Like the theory about the welfare state, this racial interpretation of the destruction of social capital is highly controversial and can hardly be settled within the compass of these brief remarks. Nevertheless, the basic facts are these.

First, racial differences in associational membership are not large.... On the other hand, racial differences in social trust are very large indeed, even taking into account differences in education, income, and so on. On average, during the 1972–94 period, controlling for educational differences, about 17 percent of blacks endorsed the view that "most people can be trusted," as compared to about 45 percent of whites, and about 27 percent of respondents of other races.[11] These racial differences in social trust, of course, reflect not collective paranoia, but real experiences over many generations.

Second, the erosion of social capital has affected all races.... Even more important, the pace of disengagement among whites has been uncorrelated with racial intolerance or support for segregation. Avowedly racist or segregationist whites have been no quicker to drop out of community organizations during this period than more tolerant whites.... This evidence also suggests that reversing the civil rights gains of the last 30 years would do nothing to reverse the social capital losses.

GENERATIONAL EFFECTS

Our efforts thus far to localize the sources of civic disengagement have been singularly unfruitful. The downtrends are uniform across the major categories of American society.... One notable exception to this uniformity, however, involves age. In all our statistical analyses, age is second only to education as a predictor of all forms of civic engagement and trust. Older people belong to more organizations than young people, and they are less misanthropic. Older

Americans also vote more often and read newspapers more frequently, two other forms of civic engagement closely correlated with joining and trusting.... Most observers have interpreted this pattern as a life-cycle phenomenon, and so, at first, did I.

Evidence from the General Social Survey enables us to follow individual cohorts as they age.... Startlingly, however, such an analysis, repeated for successive birth cohorts, produces virtually no evidence of such life-cycle changes in civic engagement. In fact, as various generations moved through the period between 1972 and 1994, their levels of trust and membership more often fell than rose, reflecting a more or less simultaneous decline in civic engagement among young and old alike, particularly during the second half of the 1980s. But that downtrend obviously cannot explain why, throughout the period, older Americans were always more trusting and engaged. In fact, the only reliable life-cycle effect visible in these data is a withdrawal from civic engagement very late in life, as we move through our 80s.

The central paradox posed by these patterns is this: Older people are consistently more engaged and trusting than younger people, yet we do not become more engaged and trusting as we age. What's going on here?

Time and age are notoriously ambiguous in their effects on social behavior. Social scientists have learned to distinguish three contrasting phenomena:

1. Life-cycle effects represent differences attributable to stage of life. In this case individuals change as they age, but since effects of aging are, in the aggregate, neatly balanced by the "demographic metabolism" of births and deaths, life-cycle effects produce no aggregate change. Everyone's close-focus eyesight worsens as we age, but the aggregate demand for reading glasses changes little.

2. Period effects affect all people who live through a given era, regardless of their age.[12] Period effects can produce both individual and aggregate change, often quickly and enduringly, without any age-related differences. The sharp drop in trust in government between 1965 and 1975, for example, was almost entirely this sort of period effect, as Americans of all ages changed their minds about their leaders' trustworthiness. Similarly, as just noted, a modest portion of the decline in social capital during the 1980s appears to be a period effect.

3. Generational effects, as described in Karl Mannheim's classic essay on "The Problem of Generations," represent the fact that "[i]ndividuals who belong to the same generation, who share the same year of birth, are endowed, to that extent, with a common location in the historical dimension of the social process" (Mannheim 1952, 290). Like life-cycle effects (and unlike typical period effects), generational effects show up as disparities among age groups at a single point in time, but like period effects (and unlike life-cycle effects) generational effects produce real social change, as successive generations, enduringly "imprinted" with divergent outlooks, enter and leave the population. In pure generational effects, no individual ever changes, but society does.

… Returning to our conundrum, how could older people today be more engaged and trusting, if they did not become more engaged and trusting as they aged? The key to this paradox, as David Butler and Donald Stokes (1974) observed in another context, is to ask not how old people are now but when they were young. Figure A.1 addresses this reformulated question, displaying various measures of civic engagement according to the respondents' year of birth.[13] …

THE LONG CIVIC GENERATION

In effect, Figure A.1 lines up Americans from left to right according to their date of birth, beginning with those born in the last third of the nineteenth century and continuing across to the generation of their great-grandchildren, born in the last third of the twentieth century.

As we begin moving along this queue from left to right—from those raised around the turn of the century to those raised during the Roaring Twenties, and so on—we find relatively high and unevenly rising levels of civic engagement and social trust. Then rather abruptly, however, we encounter signs of reduced community involvement, starting with men and women born in the early 1930s. Remarkably, this downward trend in joining, trusting, voting, and newspaper reading continues almost uninterruptedly for nearly 40 years. The trajectories for the various different indicators of civic engagement are strikingly parallel: each

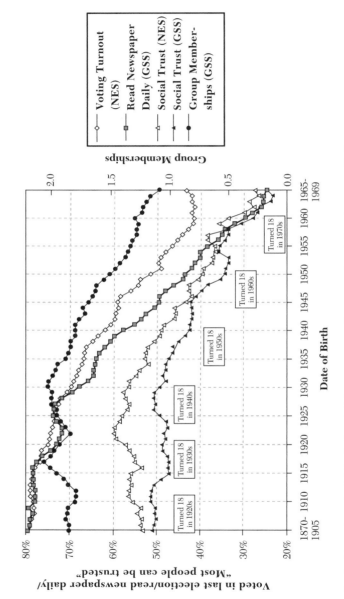

FIGURE A.1 Social Capital and Civic Engagement by Generation (education controlled)

SOURCE: General Social Survey (GSS), 1972–1994 and National Election Studies (NES), 1952–1992. Respondents aged 25–80. Five-year moving average. Equal weighting of three educational categories.

shows a high, sometimes rising plateau for people born and raised during the first third of the century; each shows a turning point in the cohorts born around 1930; and each then shows a more or less constant decline down to the cohorts born during the 1960s.[14]

By any standard, these intergenerational differences are extraordinary. Compare, for example, the generation born in the early 1920s with the generation of their grandchildren born in the late 1960s. Controlling for educational disparities, members of the generation born in the 1920s belong to almost twice as many civic associations as those born in the late 1960s (roughly 1.9 memberships per capita, compared to roughly 1.1 memberships per capita). The grandparents are more than twice as likely to trust other people (50–60 percent compared with 25 percent for the grandchildren). They vote at nearly double the rate of the most recent cohorts (roughly 75 percent compared with 40–45 percent), and they read newspapers almost three times as often (70–80 percent read a paper daily compared with 25–30 percent). And bear in mind that we have found no evidence that the youngest generation will come to match their grandparent's higher levels of civic engagement as they grow older.

Thus, read not as life-cycle effects, but rather as generational effects, the age-related patterns in our data suggest a radically different interpretation of our basic puzzle. Deciphered with this key, Figure A.1 depicts a long "civic" generation, born roughly between 1910 and 1940, a broad group of people substantially more engaged in community affairs and substantially more trusting than those younger than they.[15] The culminating point of this civic generation is the cohort born in 1925–1930, who attended grade school during the Great Depression, spent World War II in high school (or on the battlefield), first voted in 1948 or 1952, set up housekeeping in the 1950s, and watched their first television when they were in their late twenties. Since national surveying began, this cohort has been exceptionally civic: voting more, joining more, reading newspapers more, trusting more. As the distinguished sociologist Charles Tilly (born in 1928) said in commenting on an early version of this essay, "we are the last suckers."

To help in interpreting the historical contexts within which these successive generations of Americans matured, Figure A.1 also indicates the decade within which each cohort came of age. Thus, we can see that each generation that reached adulthood since the 1940s has been less engaged in community affairs than its immediate predecessor.

Further confirmation of this generational interpretation comes from a comparison of the two parallel lines that chart responses to an identical question about social trust, posed first in the National Election Studies (mainly between 1964 and 1976) and then in the General Social Survey between 1972 and 1994.[16] If the greater trust expressed by Americans born earlier in the century represented a life-cycle effect, then the graph from the GSS surveys (conducted when these cohorts were, on average, ten years older) should have been some distance above the NES line. In fact, the GSS line lies about 5–10 percent below the NES line. That downward shift almost surely represents a period effect that depressed social trust among all cohorts during the 1980s.[17] That downward period effect, however, is substantially more modest than the large generational differences already noted.

In short, the most parsimonious interpretation of the age-related differences in civic engagement is that they represent a powerful reduction in civic engagement among Americans who came of age in the decades after World War II, as well as some modest additional disengagement that affected all cohorts during the 1980s. These patterns hint that being raised after World War II was a quite different experience from being raised before that watershed. It is as though the postwar generations were exposed to some mysterious X-ray that permanently and increasingly rendered them less likely to connect with the community. Whatever that force might have been, it—rather than anything that happened during the 1970s and 1980s—accounts for most of the civic disengagement that lies at the core of our mystery....

THE PUZZLE REFORMULATED

To say that civic disengagement in contemporary America is in large measure generational merely reformulates our central puzzle. We now know that much of the cause of our lonely bowling probably dates to the 1940s and 1950s, rather than to the 1960s and 1970s. What could have been the mysterious anti-civic "X-ray" that affected Americans who came of age after World War II and whose effects progressively deepened at least into the 1970s?[18] ...

I have discovered only one prominent suspect against whom circumstantial evidence can be mounted.... The culprit is television.

First, the timing fits. The long civic generation was the last cohort of Americans to grow up without television, for television flashed into American society like lightning in the 1950s. In 1950 barely 10 percent of American homes had television sets, but by 1959 90 percent did, probably the fastest diffusion of a technological innovation ever recorded. The reverberations from this lightning bolt continued for decades, as viewing hours per capita grew by 17–20 percent during the 1960s and by an additional 7–8 percent during the 1970s. In the early years, TV watching was concentrated among the less educated sectors of the population, but during the 1970s the viewing time of the more educated sectors of the population began to converge upward. Television viewing increases with age, particularly upon retirement, but each generation since the introduction of television has begun its life cycle at a higher starting point. By 1995, viewing per TV household was more than 50 percent higher than it had been in the 1950s.[19]

Most studies estimate that the average American now watches roughly four hours per day.[20] Robinson (1990b), using the more conservative time-budget technique for determining how people allocate their time, offers an estimate closer to three hours per day, but concludes that as a primary activity, television absorbs 40 percent of the average American's free time, an increase of about one-third since 1965. Moreover, multiple sets have proliferated: by the late 1980s, three quarters of all U.S. homes had more than one set (Comstock 1989), and these numbers too are rising steadily, allowing ever more private viewing. In short, as Robinson and Godbey (1995) conclude, "television is the 800-pound gorilla of leisure time." This massive change in the way Americans spend our days and nights occurred precisely during the years of generational civic disengagement.

Evidence of a link between the arrival of television and the erosion of social connections is, however, not merely circumstantial. The links between civic engagement and television viewing can instructively be compared with the links between civic engagement and newspaper reading. The basic contrast is straightforward: newspaper reading is associated with high social capital, TV viewing with low social capital.

Controlling for education, income, age, race, place of residence, work status, and gender, TV viewing is strongly and negatively related to social trust and group membership. Figure A.1 shows that controlling for education, heavy viewers are more likely to be loners.
...

In other words, each hour spent viewing television is associated with less social trust and less group membership....

How might television destroy social capital?

- Time displacement. Even though there are only 24 hours in everyone's day, most forms of social and media participation are positively correlated. People who listen to lots of classical music are more likely, not less likely, than others to attend Cubs games. Television is the principal exception to this generalization—the only leisure activity that seems to inhibit participation outside the home. TV watching comes at the expense of nearly every social activity outside the home, especially social gatherings and informal conversations (Comstock et al. 1978; Comstock 1989; Bower 1985; and Robinson and Godbey 1995). TV viewers are homebodies....

- One important quasi-experimental study of the introduction of television in three Canadian towns (Williams 1986) found the same pattern at the aggregate level across time: a major effect of television's arrival was the reduction in participation in social, recreational, and community activities among people of all ages. In short, television is privatizing our leisure time.

- Effects on the outlooks of viewers. An impressive body of literature, gathered under the rubric of the "mean world effect," suggests that heavy watchers of TV are unusually skeptical about the benevolence of other people—overestimating crime rates, for example. This body of literature has generated much debate about the underlying causal patterns, with skeptics suggesting that misanthropy may foster couch potato behavior rather than the reverse. While awaiting better experimental evidence, however, a reasonable interim judgment is that heavy television watching may well increase pessimism about human nature (Gerbner et al. 1980; Dobb and MacDonald 1979; Hirsh 1980; and Comstock 1989, 265–69)....

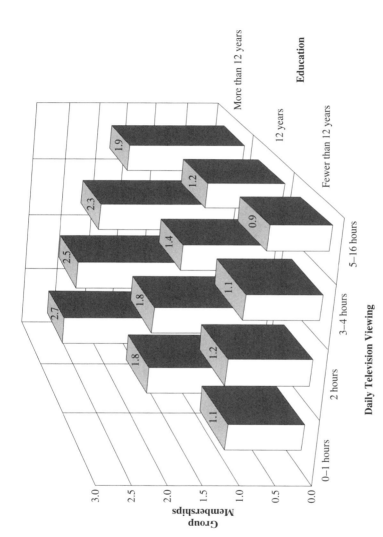

FIGURE A.2 Group Membership by Television Viewing and Education

SOURCE: General Social Survey, 1974–1994.

- Effects on children. TV occupies an extraordinary part of children's lives—consuming about 40 hours per week on average. Viewing is especially high among pre-adolescents, but it remains high among younger adolescents: time-budget studies (Carnegie Council on Adolescent Development 1993, 5, citing Timmer et al. 1985) suggest that among youngsters aged 9–14, television consumes as much time as all other discretionary activities combined, including playing, hobbies, clubs, outdoor activities, informal visiting, and just hanging out. The effects of television on childhood socialization have, of course, been hotly debated for more than three decades. The most reasonable conclusion from a welter of sometimes conflicting results appears to be that heavy television watching probably increases aggressiveness (although perhaps not actual violence), that it probably reduces school achievement, and that it is statistically associated with "psychosocial malfunctioning," although how much of this effect is self-selection and how much causal remains much debated (Condry 1993). The evidence is, as I have said, not yet enough to convict, but the defense has a lot of explaining to do.

CONCLUSION

Ithiel de Sola Pool's posthumous book *Technologies Without Borders* (1990) is a prescient work, astonishingly relevant to our current national debates about the complicated links among technology, public policy, and culture. Pool defended what he called "soft technological determinism." Revolutions in communications technologies have profoundly affected social life and culture, as the printing press helped bring on the Reformation. Pool concluded that the electronic revolution in communications technology, whose outlines he traced well before most of us were even aware of the impending changes, was the first major technological advance in centuries that would have a profoundly decentralizing and fragmenting effect on society and culture.

Pool hoped that the result might be "community without contiguity." As a classic liberal, he welcomed the benefits of technological change for individual freedom, and, in part, I share that enthusiasm. Those of us who bemoan the decline of community in contemporary America need to be sensitive to the liberating gains achieved during the same decades. We need to avoid an uncritical nostalgia for the Fifties. On the other hand, some of the same freedom-friendly technologies whose rise Pool predicted may indeed be undermining our connections with one another and with our communities. I suspect that Pool would have been open to that argument, too, for one of Pool's most talented protégés, Samuel Popkin (1991, 226–31), has argued that the rise of television and the correlative decline of social interaction have impaired American political discourse. The last line in Pool's last book (1990, 262) is this: "We may suspect that [the technological trends that we can anticipate] will promote individualism and will make it harder, not easier, to govern and organize a coherent society."

Pool's technological determinism was "soft" precisely because he recognized that social values can condition the effects of technology. In the end this perspective invites us not merely to consider how technology is privatizing our lives—if, as it seems to me, it is—but to ask whether we entirely like the result, and if not, what we might do about it. But that is a topic for another day.

REFERENCES

Bower, Robert T. 1985. *The Changing Television Audience in America*. New York: Columbia University Press.

Brehm, John, and Wendy Rahn. 1995. "An Audit of the Deficit in Social Capital." Durham, NC: Duke University. Unpublished manuscript.

Butler, David, and Donald Stokes. 1974. *Political Change in Britain: The Evolution of Electoral Choice*, 2nd ed. New York: St. Martin's.

Caplow, Theodore, Howard M. Bahr, John Modell, and Bruce A. Chadwick. 1991. *Recent Social Trends in the United States: 1960–1990*. Montreal: McGill-Queen's University Press.

Carnegie Council on Adolescent Development. 1993. *A Matter of Time: Risk and Opportunity in the Nonschool Hours: Executive Summary*. NewYork: Carnegie Corporation of New York.

Coleman, James. 1990. *Foundations of Social Theory*. Cambridge, MA: Harvard University Press.

Comstock, George. 1989. *The Evolution of American Television*. Newbury Park, CA: Sage.

Comstock, George, Steven Chaffee, Natan Katzman, Maxwell McCombs, and Donald Roberts. 1978. *Television and Human Behavior*. New York: Columbia University Press.

Condry, John. 1993. "Thief of Time, Unfaithful Servant: Television and the American Child." *Daedalus* 122 (Winter): 259–78.

Converse, Philip E. 1976. *The Dynamics of Party Support: Cohort-Analyzing Party Identification*. Beverly Hills, CA: Sage.

Cutler, Blaine. 1990. "Where Does the Free Time Go?" *American Demographics* (November): 36–39.

Davis, James Allan, and Tom W. Smith. *General Social Surveys, 1972–1994*. [machine readable data file]. Principal Investigator, James A. Davis; Director and Co-Principal Investigator, Tom W. Smith. NORC ed. Chicago: National Opinion Research Center, producer, 1994; Storrs, CT: The Roper Center for Public Opinion Research, University of Connecticut, distributor.

Dobb, Anthony N., and Glenn F. Macdonald. 1979. "Television Viewing and Fear of Victimization: Is the Relationship Causal?" *Journal of Personality and Social Psychology* 37: 170–79.

Edwards, Patricia Klobus, John N. Edwards, and Ann DeWitt Watts, "Women, Work, and Social Participation." *Journal of Voluntary Action Research* 13 (January–March, 1984), 7–22.

Elazar, Daniel J. 1966. *American Federalism: A View from the States*. New York: Crowell.

Fukuyama, Francis. 1995. *Trust: The Social Virtues and the Creation of Prosperity*. New York: The Free Press.

Gerbner, George, Larry Gross, Michael Morgan, and Nancy Signorielli. 1980. "The 'Mainstreaming' of America: Violence Profile No. 11." *Journal of Communication* 30 (Summer): 10–28.

Ginzberg, Eli. 1943. *The Unemployed*. New York: Harper and Brothers.

Glenn, Norval D. 1987. "Social Trends in the United States: Evidence from Sample Surveys." *Public Opinion Quarterly* 51: S109–S126.

Grabner, Doris A. 1993. *Mass Media and American Politics*. Washington, DC: CQ Press.

Hirsch, Paul M. 1980. "The 'Scary World' of the Nonviewer and Other Anomalies: A Reanalysis of Gerbner et al.'s Findings on Cultivation Analysis, Part I." *Communication Research* 7 (October): 403–56.

Hughes, Michael. 1980. "The Fruits of Cultivation Analysis: A Reexamination of the Effects of Television Watching on Fear of Victimization, Alienation, and the Approval of Violence." *Public Opinion Quarterly* 44: 287–303.

Jahoda, Marie, Paul Lazarsfeld, and Hans Zeisel. 1933. *Marienthal*. Chicago: Aldine-Atherton.

Mannheim, Karl. 1952. "The Problem of Generations." In *Essays on the Sociology of Knowledge*, ed. Paul Kécskemeti. New York: Oxford University Press: 276–322.

Meyrowitz, Joshua. 1985. *No Sense of Place: The Impact of Electronic Media on Social Behavior*. New York: Oxford University Press.

Miller, Warren E. 1992. "The Puzzle Transformed: Explaining Declining Turnout." *Political Behaviour* 14: 1–43.

Miller, Warren F., and J. Merrill Shanks. 1995. *The American Voter Reconsidered*. Tempe, AZ: Arizona State University. Unpublished manuscript.

Pool, Ithiel de Sola. 1973. "Public Opinion." In *Handbook of Communication*, ed. Ithiel de Sola Pool et al. Chicago: Rand McNally: 779–835.

Pool, Ithiel de Sola. 1990. *Technologies Without Boundaries: On Telecommunications in a Global Age*. Cambridge, MA: Harvard University Press.

Popkin, Samuel L. 1991. *The Reasoning Voter*. Chicago: University of Chicago Press.

Postman, Neil. 1985. *Amusing Ourselves to Death: Public Discourse in the Age of Show Business*. New York: Viking-Penguin Books.

Public Perspective. 1995. "People, Opinion, and Polls: American Popular Culture." 6 (August/September): 37–48.

Putnam, Robert D. 1993. *Making Democracy Work: Civic Traditions in Modern Italy.* Princeton, NJ: Princeton University Press.

Putnam, Robert D. 1995. "Bowling Alone, Revisited." *The Responsive Community* (Spring): 18–33.

Putnam, Robert D. 1996. "Bowling Alone: Democracy in America at the End of the Twentieth Century." In *Democracy's Victory and Crisis* by Axel Hadenius. New York: Cambridge University Press.

Robinson, John. 1981. "Television and Leisure Time: A New Scenario." *Journal of Communication* 31 (Winter): 120–130.

Robinson, John. 1990a. "The Time Squeeze." *American Demographics* (February).

Robinson, John. 1990b. "I Love My TV." *American Demographics* (September): 24–27.

Robinson, John, and Geoffrey Godbey. 1995. *Time for Life.* College Park, MD: University of Maryland. Unpublished manuscript.

Rosenstone, Steven J., and John Mark Hansen. 1993. *Mobilization, Participation, and Democracy in America.* New York: Macmillan.

Salisbury, Robert H. 1985. "Blame Dismal World Conditions on … Baseball." *Miami Herald* (May 18): 27A.

Schor, Juliet. 1991. *The Overworked American.* New York: Basic Books.

Sharkansky, Ira. 1969. "The Utility of Elazar's Political Culture." *Polity* 2: 66–83.

The Economist. 1995. "The Solitary Bowler." 334 (18 February): 21–22.

Timmer, S. G., J. Eccles, and I. O'Brien. 1985. "How Children Use Time." In *Time, Goods, and Well-Being*, ed. F. T. Juster and F. B. Stafford. Ann Arbor, MI: University of Michigan, Institute for Social Research.

U.S. Bureau of the Census. 1995 (and earlier years). *Current Population Reports.* Washington, DC.

Verba, Sidney, Kay Lehman Schlozman, and Henry E. Brady. 1995. *Voice and Equality: Civic Volunteerism in American Politics.* Cambridge, MA: Harvard University Press.

Wilcock, Richard, and Walter H. Franke. 1963. *Unwanted Workers*. New York: Free Press of Glencoe.

Williams, Tannis Macbeth, ed. 1986. *The Impact of Television: A Natural Experiment in Three Communities*. New York: Academic Press.

ABOUT THE AUTHOR

Robert D. Putnam is Clarence Dillon Professor of International Affairs and Director, Center for International Affairs, Harvard University. His 1993 book *Making Democracy Work: Civic Traditions in Modern Italy* (Princeton University Press) won the 1994 Gregory Luebber Award from the Comparative Politics Organized Section of the APSA.

NOTES

1. In this respect I deviate slightly from James Coleman's "functional" definition of social capital. See Coleman (1990): 300–321.

2. The results reported in this paragraph and throughout the paper, unless otherwise indicated, are derived from the General Social Survey.

3. Across the 35 countries for which data are available from the World Values Survey (1990–91), the correlation between the average number of associational memberships and endorsement of the view that "most people can be trusted" is $r = 65$.

4. Trust in political authorities—and indeed in many social institutions—has also declined sharply over the last three decades, but that is conceptually a distinct trend. As we shall see later, the etiology of the slump in social trust is quite different from the etiology of the decline in political trust.

5. For reasons explained below, Figure A.1 reports trends for membership in various types of groups *controlling for* the respondent's education level.

6. The only exceptions are farm groups, labor unions, and veterans' organizations, whose members have slightly less formal education than the average American.

7. This is true with or without controls for education and year of survey. The patterns among men and women on this score are not identical, for women who work part-time appear to be somewhat more civically engaged and socially trusting than either those who work full-time or those who do not work outside the home at all. Whatever we make of this intriguing anomaly, which apparently does not appear in the time budget data (Robinson and Godbey 1995) and which has no counterpart in the male half of the population, it cannot account for our basic puzzle, since female part-time workers constitute a relatively small fraction of the American population, and the fraction is growing, not declining. Between the first half of the 1970s and the first half of

the 1990s, according to the GSS data, the fraction of the total adult population constituted by female part-time workers rose from about 8 percent to about 10 percent.

8. Robinson and Godbey (1995), however, report that nonemployed women still spend more time on activity in voluntary associations than their employed counterparts.

9. Multivariate analysis hints that one major reason why divorce lowers connectedness is that it lowers family income, which in turn reduces civic engagement.

10. I have set aside this issue for fuller treatment in later work. However, I note for the record that (1) state-level differences in social trust and group membership are substantial, closely intercorrelated and reasonably stable, at least over the period from the 1970s to the 1990s, and (2) those differences are suprisingly closely correlated (R^2 = .52) with the measure of "state political culture" invented by Elazar (1966), and refined by Sharkansky (1969), based on descriptive accounts of state politics during the 1950s and traceable in turn to patterns of immigration during the nineteenth century and before.

11. As elsewhere in this essay, "controlling for educational differences" here means averaging the average scores for respondents with fewer than 12 years of schooling, with exactly 12 years, and with more than 12 years, respectively.

12. Period effects that affect only people of a specific age shade into generational effects, which is why Converse (1976), when summarizing these agerelated effects, refers to "two-and-a-half" types, rather than the conventional three types.

13. To exclude the life-cycle effects in the last years of life, Figure A.1 excludes respondents over 80. To avoid well-known problems in reliably sampling young adults, as discussed by Converse (1976), Figure A.1 also excludes respondents aged under 25. To offset the relatively small year-by-year samples and to control for educational differences, Figure A.1 charts five-year moving averages across the three educational categories used in this essay.

14. I learned of the Miller/Shanks argument only after discovering generational differences in civic engagement in the General Social Survey data, but their findings and mine are strikingly consistent.

15. Too few respondents born in the late nineteenth century appear in surveys conducted in the 1970s and 1980s for us to discern differences among successive birth cohorts with great reliability. However, those scant data (not broken out in Figure A.1) suggest that the turn of the century might have been an era of rising civic engagement. Similarly, too few respondents born after 1970 have yet appeared in national surveys for us to be confident about their distinctive generational profile, although the slender results so far seem to suggest that the 40-year generational plunge in civic engagement might be bottoming out. However, even if this turns out to be true, it will be several decades before that development could arrest the aggregate drop in civic engagement, for reasons subsequently explained in the text.

16. Members of the 1910–1940 generation also seem more civic than their elders, at least to judge by the outlooks of the relatively few men and women born in the late nineteenth century who appeared in our samples.

17. The questions on social trust appeared biennially in the NES from 1964 to 1976 and then reappeared in 1992. I have included the 1992 NES interviews in the analysis in order to obtain estimates for cohorts too young to have appeared in the earlier surveys.

18. Additional analysis of indicators of civic engagement in the GSS, not reported in detail here, confirms this downward shift during the 1980s.

19. I record here one theory attributed variously to Robert Salisbury (1985), Gerald Gamm, and Simon and Garfunkel. Devotees of our national pastime will recall that Joe Dimaggio signed with the Yankees in 1936, just as the last of the long civic generation was beginning to follow the game, and he turned center field over to Mickey Mantle in 1951, just as the last of "the suckers" reached legal maturity. Almost simultaneously, the Braves, the Athletics, the Browns, the Senators, the Dodgers, and the Giants deserted cities that had been their homes since the late nineteenth century. By the time Mantle in turn left the Yankees in 1968, much of the damage to civic loyalty had been done. This interpretation explains why Mrs. Robinson's plaintive query that year about Joltin' Joe's whereabouts evoked such widespread emotion. A deconstructionist analysis of social capital's decline would highlight the final haunting lamentation, "our nation turns its *lonely* eyes to you" [emphasis added].

20. For introductions to the massive literature on the sociology of television, see Bower (1985), Comstock et al. (1978), Comstock (1989), and Grabner (1993). The figures on viewing hours in the text are from Bower (1985, 33) and *Public Perspective* (1995, 47). Cohort differences are reported in Bower 1985, 46.

Appendix B

Trust in Government: The United States in Comparative Perspective

TODD DONOVAN
Department of Political Science,
Western Washington University

DAVID DENEMARK
Department of Political Science and International
Relations, University of Western Australia

SHAUN BOWLER
Department of Political Science, University of
California–Riverside

INTRODUCTION

How do Americans' attitudes about government and democratic politics compare to attitudes of citizens in other economically advanced democracies? As we demonstrate below, many Americans are somewhat cynical when asked if their government will do what is right "most of the time." Yet Americans display relatively high levels of trust in government when compared to citizens in most of the world's other major democracies. Why is this, and what are the effects of high (or low) levels of national trust in government? One traditional explanation of trust emphasizes the role of history and culture. That is, trust in government may be rooted in deep, long-term forces. Nations with a common history or culture, then, should have similar levels of trust in government. Our comparative analysis of trust in 29 democracies suggests that this traditional explanation may be insufficient. We find that a great deal of cross-national variation in trust can be explained by how democratic institutions perform.

The United States' experience with democracy is, in many ways, rather unique. Many of the world's established democracies have less practice with competitive democratic elections, and few have enjoyed as much stability in constitutional arrangements and partisan alignments as the United States. The large continental European democracies have had their democratic institutions and party systems uprooted in the 20th century by war and fascism, and military occupation. Other democracies have consolidated their political institutions and developed competitive party systems quite recently. The United States may also be atypical in having experienced less party system change than other democracies.

This relatively unique political history may serve to promote distinctive patterns of attitudes about democratic government, citizenship, and participation. By comparing Americans' attitudes about politics to those held by citizens in other nations, we may gain a better understanding of what is and is not unique about the American experience. Such comparisons can also illuminate the factors that cause citizens to participate in politics and to trust or distrust democratic arrangements.

TRUST AND DISTRUST OF GOVERNMENT

David Easton's (1965) classic "system theory" of politics argues that the legitimacy of democratic political systems depends on how much citizens trust their government to do what is right most of the time. In theory, political trust links people to institutions that represent them, enhancing the legitimacy and effectiveness of democratic government (Gamson, 1968; Putnam, 1993; Hetherington, 1998). Low trust and cynicism among a few people or among many people for a short period of time is to be expected and may even be healthy as a means of promoting change. The legitimacy of a regime may be endangered, however, when most people distrust their government for extended periods of time (Erber & Lau, 1990), leading to contempt for laws and support for radical (or antidemocratic) alternatives. One component of political trust may reflect support for the institutions of a political system itself (rather than the government of the day), meaning that low trust could be associated with antisystem behavior (Muller & Jukman, 1977).

One of the more striking findings from contemporary studies of public attitudes about government and politics is the low level of trust of government in many Western democracies (e.g., Dalton, 1999; Klingemann, 1999). Some observers see distrust of government as symptomatic of a general malaise among citizens of the world's established democracies. This malaise has been described in many forms. The world's wealthiest nations, having longstanding practice with representative democracy, are seen as having a crisis of trust in government, elected officials, and perhaps traditional models of democracy. Signs of this deficit of political trust have corresponded with a decline in mass attachment to established parties, the rise of "antiestablishment" parties, and declining levels of participation at elections in many nations.

Scholars of public opinion note that most citizens of Europe and North America do not trust their government to "do the right thing" most of the time. As we see below, there is substantial argument about the meaning of this, and about causes of low levels of trust in government. There is a general sense, however, that people trust their governments less today than in previous decades. There is also evidence that citizens have less confidence in the responsiveness of their governments compared to their peers 40 years ago (Nye et al., 1997; Dalton, 1988, p. 231). Early evidence of reduced political trust led many to worry that some nations could eventually experience crises of support for their democratic systems due to an erosion of the legitimacy of the regime (Miller, 1974). Conversely, if rising levels of distrust merely reflect disdain caused by scandals or dissatisfaction with incumbent politicians, not with political institutions themselves, then low levels of political discontent would be less worrisome and might be reversed (Citrin, 1974). There is little evidence, however, that there has been any increase in trust in government since low levels were identified in the 1970s. Nor is there much to suggest that the world's major democracies have experienced massive crises in regime legitimacy. All told, then, our review of Americans' trust in government can be seen against a backdrop of eroding support for government in many Western democracies, the full implications of which remain points of ongoing debate.

Surveys conducted in 2004 and 2005 in 29 of the world's most established democracies[1] (reported in Table B.1) illustrate that in all but one nation (Denmark), most respondents did not agree that "most of the time, we can trust people in government to do what is right." Nonetheless, the United States rates as one of the most trusting nations, with just 10 other affluent democracies showing higher levels of public trust in government. In nations with the highest levels of trust, 40 to 55 percent trust their government. In Poland, Germany, Slovakia, and Japan, in contrast, only 1 in 10 respondents expresses such trust.

There is some evidence that trust has eroded in many of these nations since the 1970s. When opinions from the 2004 ISSP surveys are compared to similar measures taken in the mid-1970s, we find evidence of a decline in political trust and confidence in a number of nations where comparable data are available. Fewer Americans, British, French, and Germans expressed trust in their government or confidence in public officials in 2004 than in the late 1970s. Dalton (1988, p. 232) reported 34 percent of Americans, 40 percent of British, and 52 percent of West Germans trusted government "to do right" in 1977—higher levels of trust than displayed in Table B.1. Dalton also reported 43 percent of Americans, 31 percent of British, 36 percent of French, and 34 percent of West Germans said government officials "cared" what people think in 1977. The 2004 ISSP survey found lower confidence in officials in each of these nations: 35 percent of Americans, 23 percent of British, 27 percent of French, and just 10 percent of unified Germans held this opinion. Studies of Canada (Kornberg & Clarke, 1992), Finland (Borg & Sankiaho, 1995), and Sweden (Holmberg, 1999) all find declining trust. Trust may also be in decline in Britain, Italy, and Japan (Dalton, 1999; Beer, 1982).

When results in Table B.1 are compared to previous studies, there is less evidence of erosion of trust in Denmark and the Netherlands (Listhaug & Wiberg, 1995; Newton & Norris, 2000)—a pattern that echoes their high levels of satisfaction with democracy (Lijphart, 1999, p. 286).

T A B L E   B.1   Trust in Government, 2004

	Respondent Opinion (%)*	Label in Figures
Denmark	55	dn
Finland	46	fn
Switzerland	46	swi
Cyprus	41	cy
Australia	40	au
New Zealand	40	nz
Chile	38	cl
Canada	37	cn
Sweden	36	swe
Spain	33	sp
United States	31	us
Netherlands	29	ne
Great Britain	29	gb
Norway	27	no
Portugal	26	pr
Slovenia	26	svn
Belgium (Flan)	24	bl
South Korea	23	sk
Hungary	23	hn
Israel	23	is
France	22	fr
Austria	19	as
Czech Republic	19	cz
Latvia	19	lt
Taiwan	15	tw
Poland	11	pl
Germany	10	ge
Slovakia	10	svk
Japan	9	jp

*This is the percent of respondents in each nation who strongly agree or agree to the statement: "Most of the time we can trust people in government to do what is right."

SOURCE: ISSP Citizenship Module, 2004.

Australia may also be one of the few established democracies where political trust is not in decline. Compared to people in most other affluent democracies in 2004, Australians are relatively trusting of their government, with 40 percent saying government can be trusted to do what is right. Although few comparable surveys of Australian attitudes are available prior to the 1990s, trust may well be higher in Australia in 2004 than in previous decades. Australian surveys in 1979 and 1988, for example, found just 29 percent of Australians saying the government could be trusted to "do the right thing" (McAllister, 1992; p. 45).[2]

Figure B.1 provides evidence that, overall, trust in government corresponds with individuals' satisfaction with existing democratic arrangements—likely a reflection of their assessments of government, or regime, performance (Dalton, 1999). Trust in government and satisfaction with how democracy is working, then, can be seen to be highly correlated across the 29 democracies included in this study ($r = 0.80$). In Figure B.1, the United States' location is represented with the letters "us." In these cross-national patterns, we see that the United States ranks among the highest of these nations in terms of levels of political trust and satisfaction with how democracy is working. High levels of trust also correspond with positive assessments of democracy in Australia, New Zealand, Finland, Switzerland, and Denmark. Clearly, the other side of this coin is that low trust corresponds with dissatisfaction with how the nation's democratic system is working. Low levels of trust correspond with poor evaluations of how democracy is performing in Poland, Japan, Slovakia, and the Czech Republic.

But what do high (or low) levels of political trust really mean? What might we make of the fact that just 31 percent of American respondents trust their government? Conversely, what does it mean that few Austrians, French, and Japanese trust their government "to do what is right" most of the time? As we see below, Americans have fairly cynical assessments of politics when we consider some attitudes; but relative to citizens of many of the world's major democracies, they are quite optimistic. In the sections below, we examine various explanations for the causes of low political trust in order to assess what political attitudes correspond with political trust and distrust.

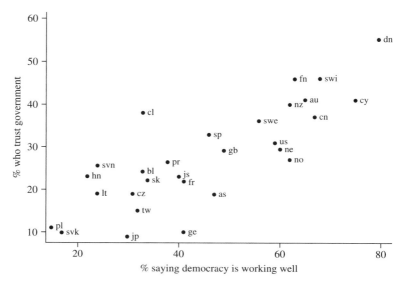

FIGURE B.1 Trust Government to Do the Right Thing by Evaluations of How Well Democracy Works Today. [Respondents were asked: On the whole, on a scale from 0 to 10, where 0 is very poorly and 10 is very well, how well does democracy work in (COUNTRY) today? The x axis depicts the percent of respondents responding 7 or higher. r = 0.80.]

CRITICAL CITIZENS AND POLITICAL ENGAGEMENT

One influential explanation for contemporary political distrust is that the political behavior and expectations of citizens have changed over recent generations. Public expectations about how government should work and of the role of citizens in their political system may have changed substantially since World War II. With higher levels of education among the mass public, greater levels of affluence, and greater access to information, contemporary citizens may well expect a more direct say in what government does and have less interest in traditional modes of representation.

Some political analysts see the trend toward weaker party loyalties (Dalton, 1984), greater direct citizen influence over party nominations, more frequent use of citizen initiatives and referendums, and direct election of local officials as the result of popular demands for new forms of participation (Budge, 1996; LeDuc, 2003, p. 30). As democratic nations mature, citizens may come to believe they are quite capable of playing a direct role in governing while being suspicious of established political arrangements that grant significant responsibilities to elected officials. Research from Norris (1999) and Inglehart (1990) suggests that these demands come from politically cynical citizens who are losing confidence in representative government and conventional modes of politics but yet retain a strong commitment to the principles of democracy. Others note a corresponding decline in the willingness of citizens to defer to authority (Inglehart, 1990) as important in the "unfreezing" of political alignments and institutions (Bogdanor, 1994). From this perspective, because many "post-material" (Inglehart, 1977) or "critical citizens" (Norris, 1999) in the contemporary era now have most of their material needs satisfied, their orientation toward government and politics may have come to focus more on the political process itself.

In this new political relationship, as affluence and education increase, citizens are expected to demand more direct influence. However, if we look at the overall correlation between national wealth (GDP per capita) and levels of political trust, we find that, across the affluent democracies listed in Table B.1, levels of trust and levels of per capita income are only slightly related ($r = 0.30$). America lies well above the average level of national wealth per head among these nations and slightly above the average level of political trust. America's relatively high levels of political trust, then, may reflect something about its wealth, but national wealth is only a modest predictor of trust across these 29 nations.

CITIZEN INVOLVEMENT AND ENGAGEMENT

Dalton (1984) and Inglehart (1990) have emphasized that the higher levels of "cognitive mobilization" of contemporary citizens have led to greater demands for public access to governmental decisionmaking processes. The classic idea of elected representatives serving as trustees who are granted broad discretion by their constituents may have been undermined by citizens' growing expectations that elected officials should serve as delegates who directly express the will of the public. This suggests that nations where individual citizens have more internal political efficacy—that is, a sense that they have the personal capacity to understand political issues and affect government—will have higher levels of engagement with the political system. Figure B.2 illustrates that citizens who lack personal political efficacy tend to have low levels of political trust ($r = 0.46$). We see here that relatively high levels of political trust in Denmark, Switzerland, Australia, New Zealand, and Cyprus correspond with relatively high levels of personal or internal political efficacy. However, high efficacy in the United States and Belgium does not correspond with high levels of trust.

But a key element of the critical citizen/post-materialist model of citizen orientation to government centers on demands for participatory politics: in other words, high efficacy—the sense that participation in politics is important and actually matters—leads to higher expectations about the role of the citizen in a democratic society. The patterns in Figure B.3 confirm the importance of this linkage: there is a clear inverse relationship between levels of political trust and the proportion of people who feel their nation's opportunities for citizen participation are inadequate ($r = -0.44$). Here, in the

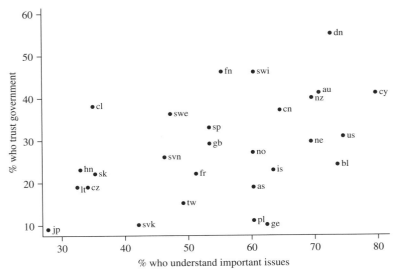

F I G U R E B.2 Trust in Government by Personal Efficacy (as measured by percent saying they understand political issues). [Efficacy measured as the percent of respondents who strongly agree or agree that "I feel I have a pretty good understanding of the important political issues facing (COUNTRY)." The x axis represents the percentage of respondents who strongly agree or disagree. $r = 0.46$.]

right-hand portion of the figure, we see lower levels of trust where citizens feel that they need more opportunities for input in decision making—nations like Japan and Germany, where opportunities for direct political participation are relatively limited (Scarrow, 2001). Higher trust is evident where people find participatory opportunities more adequate. A case in point is the high levels of trust in Switzerland, which has the most directly democratic arrangements among the world's democracies. Denmark and Sweden, with multiparty systems that may tend to promote representation and voters' sense of connectedness with their party, follow suit. Conversely, in nations where more people believe that additional modes of citizen input are required, trust is lower. Japan, for example, with a rigid party system long dominated by one party, ranks high on demands for more citizen input and low on trust in government.

This variant of the critical citizen/post-materialist thesis has been used to explain the decline of social class as a basis for party

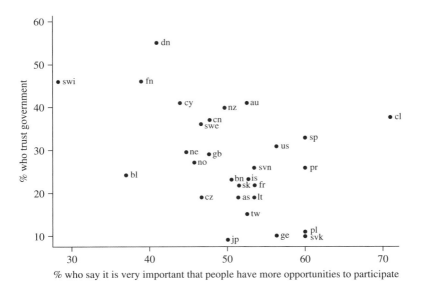

F I G U R E B.3   Trust in Government and Demands for More Citizen Involvement (as measured by percent saying it is very important that people have more opportunities to participate). [Respondents were asked: There are different opinions about people's rights in a democracy. On a scale of 1 to 7, where 1 is not important and 7 is very important, how important is it that people be given more opportunities to participate in public decision making? The *x* axis represents the percent of citizens rating more citizen involvement at 7 (that is, rating it as very important). *r* = −0.44.]

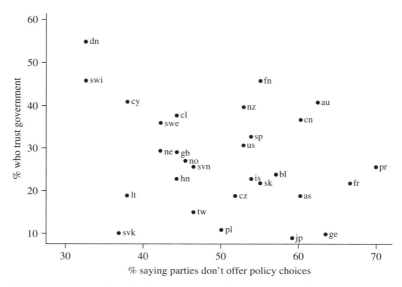

FIGURE B.4 Trust in Government and Discontent with Party Choices. [Respondents were asked: Thinking now of politics in (COUNTRY), to what extent do you agree or disagree with the statement that political parties do not really give voters real policy choices? The *x* axis plots the percent who strongly agreed and agreed. *r* = –0.30.]

support (Dalton, 1988) and the rise of support for independent candidates and nontraditional parties. In short, the expectation here is that those who feel that political parties provide inadequate choices and opportunities for involvement will be distrusting of government. And indeed, Figure B.4 illustrates that distrust is modestly associated with frustration about the choices presented by political parties ($r = -0.30$) and that most Americans agree with the statement "political parties do not give voters real policy choices." Thus, despite (or because of) the stability of the American party system, we find a level of frustration with political parties in America similar to that in Israel and South Korea.

CORRUPTION, CYNICISM, AND POLITICAL DISTRUST

Another explanation for the current state of citizen orientation toward government and politics is that changes in the availability of political information have made people more aware of what their governments do, but that there are ill effects of this new awareness.

In previous generations, citizens may have been socialized to have a sense of blind loyalty to their party and government, and a willingness to participate flowing from a sense of civic duty. But the rise of the mass media—with their focus on scandal and hostile investigative reporting (Graber, 1989, p. 235)— makes it harder for governments to hide their dirty laundry. A consequence of this increased popular scrutiny of the workings of governments, and attention to scandals, may well be a reduction in citizens' confidence in political institutions (Patterson & Donsbach, 1996). If so, then current cynicism about politics reflects the unmasking of political events (e.g., Watergate, sex scandals, bribery) that would have gone unnoticed in previous generations.

Much of the attention of the mass media has been on political corruption—such as stories about disgraced lobbyist Jack Abramoff, members of Congress pleading guilty to bribery (Randy "Duke" Cunningham, R–CA), influence peddling (Bob Ney, R–OH; Richard Pombo, R–CA), the solicitation and acceptance of illegal gifts in exchange for assistance with earmarks (Allan Mollohan, D–WV), $90,000 in suspected cash bribes hidden in a Congressman's freezer (William Jefferson, D–LA), nepotism (John Doolittle, R–CA; Curt Weldon, R–PA; Richard Pombo, R–CA; and Maxine Waters, D–CA), FBI subpoenas issued to investigate lobbyist shakedown schemes (Jerry Lewis, R–CA), earmarking of public funds for personal gain (Ken Calvert, R–CA), and improper sexual e-mails (Mark Foley, R–FL). The volume of such media focus suggests that political distrust may reflect perceptions of corruption about politicians.[3]

Figure B.5 illustrates a strong negative link at the national level between trust and the idea that corruption is widespread in a nation's public service ($r = -0.60$). Our data also show a strong link between perceptions of corruption in the public service and the belief that "politicians are in politics only for what they can get out of it personally" ($r = 0.80$). Figure B.5 suggests that a relatively high proportion of Americans perceive that corruption is a problem among their public officials. Nations toward the left in Figure B.5 have fewer people who say that "a lot" or "almost everyone" in public life is corrupt; those to the right have more people saying this. There are more nations to the right of the United States (with lower public perceptions of official corruption) than to the left (where nations such as Japan and South Korea—with notoriously corrupt elected officials—are located). Figure B.5 suggests that trust in government

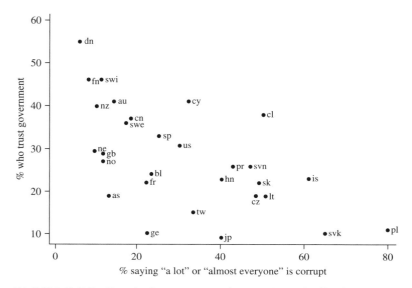

F I G U R E B.5 Trust in Government and Perceptions of Official Corruption (as measured by the percent who say "a lot" or "almost everyone" in public service is corrupt). [Respondents were asked: How widespread do you think corruption is in the public service in (COUNTRY)? Response categories included "Hardly anyone is involved; a small number of people are involved; a moderate number of people are involved; a lot of people are involved; almost everyone is involved." The x axis plots the percent of respondents who replied "a lot of people" or "almost everyone." r = –0.60.]

in the United States and across these 29 nations may be shaped by perceptions of how well (or badly) public officials behave. Indeed, the lowest levels of trust are found in nations known to have relatively high levels of corruption among bureaucrats and public officials (e.g., Poland and Slovakia, which have high levels of corruption according to Transparency International).

There is some debate about the meaning of this link between perceptions of corruption and trust. It may reflect how democratic institutions are actually functioning (or failing to function); or it may reflect media-fueled cynicism, which has little grounding in how politicians and public officials actually (mis)behave. That said, survey research in several nations has demonstrated that citizens in places with higher levels of public corruption have more negative attitudes about public officials and less trust in government (Anderson & Tverdova, 2003). Personal exposure to acts of official corruption has also been shown to erode confidence in the political system and to lower interpersonal trust (Seligson, 2002). Putnam (1993) demonstrated strong links between political attitudes and government performance in Italy. Behavioral studies also find that people who are represented by legislators caught in scandals have lower trust and political cynicism, and that voter experience with actual scandals, rather than just exposure to news, drives cynicism (Bowler & Karp, 2004).

All of this leads us to believe that patterns of opinion plotted in Figure B.5 probably reflect something about how actual corrupt practices might compromise trust in democracy. For one thing, an external measure of corruption in each nation derived from assessments of experts, businesspeople, and international organizations (the Transparency International Corruption Perceptions Index, or CPI) is strongly correlated with our survey respondents' perceptions of public corruption in their nations ($r = 0.82$). Perceptions of corruption measured in the ISSP surveys are also highly correlated with World Bank measures of the quality of a nation's regulatory system (-0.78) and governmental effectiveness (-0.90). Furthermore, we see that people in Japan and South Korea, where massive bribery scandals have rocked governments, are more likely to perceive public officials as corrupt. People in Portugal and the Czech Republic, with the lowest CPI ranking of the nations in our study, have the highest reported perceptions of corruption. Finland and Denmark, ranked as the world's two cleanest political systems, have citizens with the lowest perceptions of official corruption.

Perceptions of corruption—and actual corruption—are also important, as they probably affect trust by conditioning attitudes about the responsiveness of government. Figure B.6 illustrates a strong negative relationship between national levels of trust in government and perceptions that government "doesn't care much about what people like me think" ($r = -0.72$). This sentiment—that government doesn't care—is associated with perceptions of public corruption ($r = 0.57$). We also find these feelings regarding government's unresponsiveness associated with the objective corruption index (CPI) measure ($r = 0.52$).

THE ROLE OF SOCIAL CAPITAL

Social forces, as well as these political factors, might affect national levels of trust in government. Many commentators have promoted

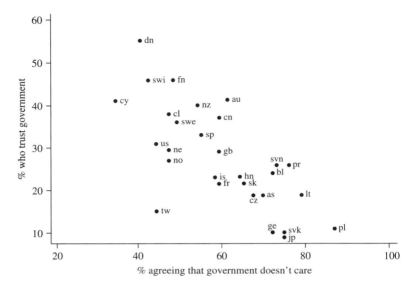

FIGURE B.6 Trust in Government and Perceptions of Governmental Responsiveness (as measured by the percent who say they don't think government cares about "people like me"). [The x axis plots the percent of respondents who agreed or strongly agreed with the statement: I don't think government cares much what people like me think. r = –0.72.]

the idea that the health of a political system flows from social capital—a macro-level resource that enhances a polity's ability to act collectively (Coleman, 1990, p. 302). Drawing on de Tocqueville, Robert Putnam (2000) defines social capital as the "norms of reciprocity and trust" arising out of social networks and voluntary associations. People may learn how to act collectively as citizens, learn "public-spiritedness," and learn to trust others in part by joining and participating in voluntary groups such as sports clubs, church groups, arts clubs, and the like (Verba, et al., 1995). Early comparative studies of mass attitudes about democracy (Almond & Verba, 1963) noted the importance of civic volunteerism.

Newton and Norris (2000) also found aggregate levels of social trust and confidence in government to be strongly associated in 17 "trilateral democracies." Echoing Putnam (1993), they argue that social trust can build effective social and political institutions, which, in turn, help government perform better and encourage confidence in government. Social participation in arts clubs, choir groups, sports clubs, and other voluntary groups is associated with political engagement and participation in Europe (Bowler et al, 2003) and New Zealand (Donovan et al., 2004). Studies suggest that membership in voluntary associations is in decline (Putnam, 1995). Low rates of participation in voluntary groups may correspond with less social capital, less trust, and less political activity. Putnam suggests that high levels of political cynicism and distrust may be the effect of an erosion of social capital—an erosion he attributes to people now spending their leisure time watching TV rather than working with others in groups.

Bean (2001, 2005) demonstrates that social or interpersonal trust appears to be a better indicator of social capital than political trust (or trust in government), and that social trust promotes political participation. Indeed, social capital theory holds that trust of other people is a prerequisite for trust in government and that trust in people is learned via activity in voluntary nonpolitical groups.

Figure B.7 illustrates the first part of the relationship between social group activity and interpersonal trust. Here we see evidence that participation in social groups is associated with more interpersonal trust at the national level—with trust now measured by the percentage of people in a nation who report that other people can always or usually be trusted. Interpersonal trust is greater in nations where more people interact with each other in sports groups ($r = 0.57$). Levels of interpersonal trust are also higher in countries where more people participate in other (unnamed) voluntary associations ($r = 0.46$). Additional analysis of the cross-national data reveals that nations with higher rates of participation in sports, leisure, and cultural groups have fewer people reporting that they feel taken advantage of by other people ($r = -0.72$). Higher participation in church groups, in contrast, has no clear relationship with a nation's stock of interpersonal trust ($r = -0.05$).

Figure B.8 demonstrates the second part of the social capital thesis: the relationship between interpersonal trust and trust in government. Here we see that nations with more people who trust other people tend to have higher levels of trust in government ($r = 0.60$). Part of America's relatively high levels of trust in government, then, may reflect a relatively healthy stock of interpersonal trust (social capital) that is maintained by active participation in voluntary social groups, such as sports clubs and cultural groups—at least when the United States is compared to Portugal, Spain, Taiwan, Poland, Latvia, and Chile.

There are also forces that inhibit the growth of interpersonal trust. As we demonstrated above (Figure B.5), perceptions of corruption in public life both play an important role in explaining trust in

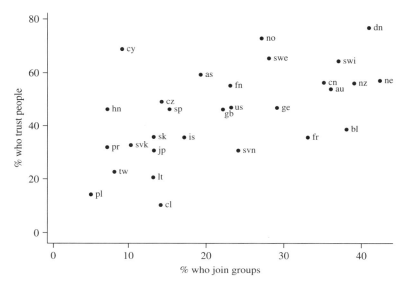

FIGURE B.7 Interpersonal Trust and Percent of People Who Are Members of Sports, Leisure, or Cultural Groups. [People were asked: People sometimes belong to different kinds of groups or associations. For each type of group, please indicate whether you belong and actively participate, belong but don't participate, used to belong but do not anymore, or have never belonged. The x axis plots the percent of people who reported belonging and actively participating in a sports, leisure, or cultural group. Data on the y axis are described in Figure B.8. $r = 0.57$.]

government. Corruption, both actual and perceived, has a corrosive effect on trust in government (Figure B.5) and on perceptions of governmental responsiveness. We also find that interpersonal trust is lower where the perception of corruption is greater ($r = -0.76$), where there is more actual corruption ($r = 0.58$), and where more people think that politicians are in office only for selfish purposes ($r = -0.78$). This likely reflects a complex causal relationship between social capital and the performance of democratic institutions reflected in Putnam's idea (1993) that democratic governments have difficulty functioning without some basic reservoir of interpersonal trust.

Citizenship and Participation

But what are the political consequences of low (or high) levels of trust in government? If trust in government also reflects general support for a political system (Muller & Jukman, 1977) or the legitimacy of a country's political system (Easton, 1965), then we

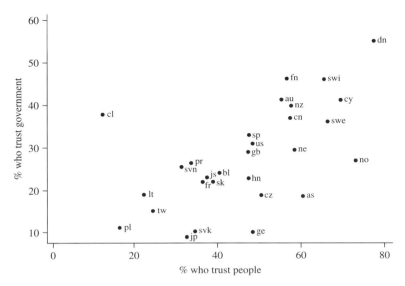

FIGURE B.8   Trust in Government and Interpersonal Trust (percent who trust other people). [Respondents were asked: Generally speaking, would you say that most people could be trusted or that you can't be too careful dealing with people? Response categories included "People can almost always be trusted; people can usually be trusted; you usually can't be too careful in dealing with people; you almost always can't be too careful in dealing with people." The x axis plots the percent of people who reported the first two responses. r = 0.60.]

should expect to see behavioral or attitudinal consequences. Public opinion data are ill-suited for measuring attitudes or behaviors that represent a serious rejection of a nation's political system (such as willingness to riot or propensity toward rebellion). However, the ISSP Citizenship module includes some measures of how people are oriented to their political system, including attitudes about how important it is that citizens obey laws and regulations and pay their taxes. These data also include measures of various modes of political participation. If trust in government does somehow represent acceptance of the legitimacy of a political system, we may expect to see that people attach more importance to obeying laws and more willingness to participate in politics in nations where more of them trust their government.

At the aggregate level, political trust is correlated with multiple forms of political participation. Trust in government across the 29 democracies corresponds with higher levels of support for the idea that citizenship requires that people always vote ($r = 0.33$), and higher trust of government in a nation corresponds with more respondents from that nation reporting voting in the last election ($r =$ 0.28). Likewise, we find that more people report "contacting or attempting to contact a politician or civil servant to express your views" in nations with higher trust in government ($r = 0.40$). This result should be considered in light of the relationship between political trust and corruption discussed above. It suggests that an ill-functioning public service not only discourages people from trusting government but also discourages them from contacting public officials. Indeed, there is a robust negative relationship between perceived corruption and the proportion of citizens in a nation who report contacting public officials ($r = -0.62$). We also find a similar correlation between the Transparency International measure of actual corruption and the percentage of people who contact officials ($r = -0.64$). Figure B.9 illustrates that citizens in nations with lower levels of trust in government also have distinct attitudes about the need for citizens to engage in civil disobedience if they oppose government actions ($r = -0.51$). Support for the idea that democracy requires citizens disobey government acts they oppose is highest in new democracies with high corruption and low trust in government (Slovakia and Poland).

Democratic Performance vs. Political Culture

We have demonstrated that trust in government depends on evaluations of how well democracy is performing, on perceptions of political efficacy, frustration with the scope of citizen input into the political system, and evaluations of governmental responsiveness. Higher levels of political trust appear to correspond with better-performing (less corrupt) political systems, and political trust is associated with social capital.

Results from these surveys of citizens in 29 democracies reveal that levels of trust in government, and interpersonal trust, vary widely across nations with similar cultures, and similar levels of trust appear in nations with vastly different histories and cultures.

Levels of trust in government found in the United States are as similar to those of Spain and the Netherlands as they are to those of Great Britain. Likewise, interpersonal trust among Americans is closer to what we find in Hungary and Germany than in New Zealand, Canada, and Australia. We find nearly identical (low) levels of trust in France and Japan. Likewise, Germany and South

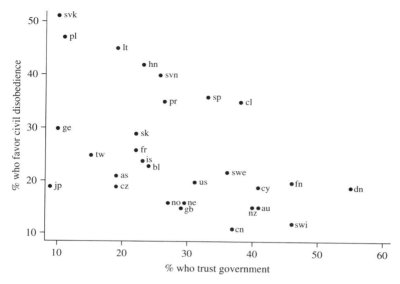

FIGURE B.9   The Need for Civil Disobedience (percent who say it is important to disobey when you disagree with government) versus Trust in Government. [The *y* axis represents the percent of respondents who responded 7 when asked: There are different opinions about what it takes to be a good citizen. As far as you are concerned personally, on a scale of 1 to 7 (with 1 not important at all and 7 very important), how important is it that citizens may engage in civil disobedience when they oppose government actions? The *x* axis is the percent who trust government. $r = -0.51$.]

Korea post nearly identical (low) levels of trust in government. Cross-national differences in social and political culture or the British influence that America shares with Australia, Canada, and New Zealand seem somewhat inadequate for explaining relatively high levels of trust found in the United States.

   These findings should offer some optimism for emerging democracies and established democracies that face a crisis of political trust, as they suggest that political outcomes and democratic performance, rather than immutable national culture, are associated with democratic prospects. Culture may be far less malleable than democratic institutions and political or economic outputs. If political trust is determined by deeply rooted cultural norms, it may take several generations to build democracies that function well. However, if trust flows from the performance of institutions, then better institutional performance (fewer scandals, less corruption) may build political trust. Likewise, the growth of participation in civil society may also build interpersonal and political trust. Governments may be able to generate trust by eliminating corruption, improving the performance of democratic institutions, and perhaps by addressing public perceptions of inadequate opportunities for citizen input.

There are, of course, other components of trust that we have not accounted for in this analysis. As stated by Anderson et al. (2005, p. 67), trust of government in America is associated with whether a person supported the party that controlled government. This result has been found in cross-national studies of trust as well, but it is a short-term effect: supporters of parties out of power come to trust government more once their party is in power. As we noted above, economic performance, measured by GDP per capita, is only weakly related to trust in government. This result may reflect the fact that the set of democracies considered here are all relatively affluent. Analysis of opinions in newer, less affluent democracies illustrates that people are more trusting of government where economic performance is stronger (Mishler & Rose, 2001). Economic performance can be seen as a system output, however. Improvements in the economy may thus offer some promise for building trust.

American Exceptionalism?

Although it is somewhat common to note that Americans are cynical about politics and that most do not trust their government, when these attitudes are examined in a cross-national perspective, Americans' assessments of democracy appear modestly optimistic. Compared to most other rich democracies, the United States experiences fairly high levels of trust in government, a public who approves of how well democracy is working, and very high levels of personal (internal) efficacy—although the effects of these things on building trust may be offset by (relatively) high levels of perceived political corruption. Nonetheless, Americans place more value on obeying laws, honesty in tax payments, and voting than citizens of most other nations examined here. We do find that Americans are slightly more likely to say that their political parties don't offer "real policy choices," and they are much more likely to say that people should be given more opportunities to participate in public decision making. This suggests that aggregate distrust of government in America is not likely a reflection of those with antisystem or antidemocratic views but rather a reflection of people who, as Dalton (1999) notes, want to risk more democracy.

Still, this begs the question of why Americans are more trusting of their government compared to Japanese, Germans, Poles, Czechs, French, Austrians, and Norwegians. Moreover, if social capital and the performance of democratic institutions (corruption) build trust in government, what has changed in the United States in the last few decades that might depress political trust? Many of the structural features that might make America exceptional—no 20th-century experience with fascism, no socialist revolution, an enduring party system, very high wealth, etc.—have not changed since lower levels of trust were measured in the 1970s and 1980s.

We can only speculate what it is about the United States that may lead to lower levels of trust today than 40 years ago. Opinions measured in 2004 may somehow reflect a period of war and memories of 9/11. Measures from previous decades may reflect less anxiety about security and terrorism. Current measures of trust in America may reflect, at least in part, a healthy economy. The American economy was certainly performing better in 2004 than in the late 1970s, and in some nations' trends in trust correspond with economic performance. In Germany, for example, trust declined as economic performance weakened after unification. It is more difficult, however, to assess if contemporary levels reflect whether democratic institutions are performing better or worse: we cannot tell if there are higher levels of perceived corruption today than before.

REFERENCES

Almond, G., & Verba, S. (1963). *The Civic Culture: Political Attitudes and Democracy in Five Nations*. Princeton, N.J.: Princeton University Press.

Anderson, C., & Tverdova, Y. (2003). "Corruption, Political Allegiances, and Attitudes Toward Government in Contemporary Democracies." *American Journal of Political Science*, 47, 91–109.

Anderson, C., Blais, A., Bowler, S., Donovan, T., & Listhaug, O. (2005). *Loser's Consent: Elections and Democratic Legitimacy*. New York: Oxford University Press.

Bean, C. (2005). "Is There a Crisis of Political Trust in Australia?" In *Australian Social Attitudes: The First Report*. New South Wales: University of New South Wales Press.

Bean, C. (2001). "Party Politics, Political Leaders and Trust in Government in Australia." *Political Science*, *53*, 17–27.

Beer, S. (1982). *Britain Against Itself*. New York: Norton.

Bogdanor, V. (1994). "Western Europe." In Butler, D., & Ranney, A. (Eds.), *Referendums Around the World*. Washington, D.C.: AEI Press.

Borg, S., & Sankiaho, R. (1995). *The Finnish Voter*. Tampere: The Finnish Political Science Association.

Bowler, S., Donovan, T., & Hanneman, R. (2003). "Art for Democracy's Sake: Social Group Membership and Civic Engagement in Europe." *Journal of Politics*, *65*(4), 1111–1129.

Bowler, S. & Karp, J. (2004) "Politicians, Scandals and Trust in Government." *Political Behavior*, *26*(3), 271–287.

Budge, I. (1996). *The New Challenge of Direct Democracy*. Cambridge, Mass.: Polity Press.

Citrin, J. (1974). "Comment: The Political Relevance of Trust in Government." *American Political Science Review*, *68*, 973–988.

Coleman, J. (1990). *Foundations of Social Theory*. Cambridge, Mass.: Harvard University Press.

Dalton, R. (1984). *Electoral Change in Advanced Industrial Democracies: Realignment or Dealignment?* Princeton, N.J.: Princeton University Press.

Dalton, R. (1988). *Citizen Politics in Western Democracies: Public Opinion and Political Parties in the United States, Great Britain, West Germany and France*. Chatham, N.J.: Chatham House.

Dalton, R. (1999). "Political Support in Advanced Industrial Democracies." In Norris, P. (Ed.), *Critical Citizens: Global Support for Democratic Governance*. Oxford, U.K.: Oxford University Press.

Donovan, T., Bowler, S., Karp, J., & Hanneman, R. (2004). "Sports, Social Group Membership and Political Engagement in New Zealand." *Australian Journal of Political Science*, *39*(2), 405–419.

Easton, D. (1965). *A Systems Analysis of Political Life*. New York: Wiley.

Erber, R., & Lau, R., (1990). "Political Cynicism Revisited." *American Journal of Political Science*, *34*(1), 263–253.

Hetherington, M. (1998). "The Political Relevance of Trust." *American Political Science Review*, *92*(4), 791–808.

Holmberg, S. (1999). In Norris, P. (Ed.), *Critical Citizens: Global Support for Democratic Governance*. Oxford, U.K.: Oxford University Press.

Gamson, W. (1968). *Power and Discontent*. Homewood, Ill.: Dorsey Press.

Graber, D. (1989). *Mass Media and American Politics*. (3rd ed). Washington, D.C.: Congressional Quarterly Press.

Inglehart, R. (1977). *Silent Revolution: Changing Values and Political Styles Among Western Publics*. Princeton, N.J.: Princeton University Press.

Inglehart, R. (1990). *Culture Shift in Advanced Industrial Society*. Princeton, N.J.: Princeton University Press.

Klingemann, H. D. (1999). In Norris, P. (Ed.), *Critical Citizens: Global Support for Democratic Governance*. Oxford, U.K.: Oxford University Press.

Kornberg, A., & Clarke, H. D. (1992). *Citizens and Community: Political Support in a Representative Democracy*. Oakleigh, Australia: Cambridge University Press.

LeDuc, L. (2003). *The Politics of Direct Democracy: Referendum in Comparative Perspective*. Toronto: Broadview Press.

Levi, M. (1996). "Social and Unsocial Capital: A Review Essay on Robert Putnam's *Making Democracy Work*." *Politics and Society*, *24*, 45–55.

Lijphart, A. (1999). *Patterns of Democracy: Government Forms and Performance in Thirty-Six Countries*. New Haven, Conn.: Yale University Press.

Listhaug, O., & Wiberg, M. (1995). "The Dynamics of Trust in Politicians." In Klingemann, H-D., & Fuchs, D. (Eds.), *Citizens and the State*. New York: Oxford University Press.

McAllister, I. (1992). *Political Behaviour: Citizens, Parties and Elites in Australia*. Melbourne: Longman Cheshire.

Miller, A. (1974). "Political Issues and Trust in Government: 1964–1970." *American Political Science Review, 68,* 951–972.

Mishler, W., & Rose, R. (2001). "What Are the Origins of Political Trust?" *Comparative Political Studies, 34,* 30–62.

Muller, E., & Jukman, T. (1977). "On the Meaning of Political Support." *American Political Science Review, 71,* 1561–1595

Newton, K., & Norris, P. (2000). "Confidence in Public Institutions: Faith, Culture or Performance." In Pharr, S. & Putnam, R. (Eds.), *What's Troubling the Trilateral Democracies?* Princeton, N.J.: Princeton University Press.

Norris, P. (1999). *Critical Citizens: Global Support for Democratic Governance.* Oxford, U.K.: Oxford University Press.

Nye, J. S., Zelikow, P. D., & King, D. C. (Eds.) (1997). *Why People Don't Trust Government.* Cambridge, Mass.: Harvard University Press.

Patterson, T. E., & Donsbach, W. (1996). "News Decisions: Journalists as Partisan Actors." *Political Communication, 13,* 455–468.

Putnam, R. (1993). *Making Democracy Work: Civic Traditions in Modern Italy.* Princeton, N.J.: Princeton University Press.

Putnam, R. (1995). "Tuning In, Tuning Out: The Strange Disappearance of Social Capital in America." *PS: Political Science and Politics, 28*(4), 644–683.

Putnam, R. (2000). *Bowling Alone: The Collapse and Revival of American Community.* New York: Simon & Schuster.

Scarrow, S. (2001). "Direct Democracy and Institutional Change." *Comparative Politics Status, 34,* 651–665.

Seligson, M. (2002). "The Impact of Corruption on Regime Legitimacy: A Comparative Study of Four Latin American Democracies." *Journal of Politics, 64,* 408–433.

Verba, S., Schlozman, K., & Brady, H. (1995). *Voice & Equality: Civic Voluntarism in American Politics.* Cambridge, Mass.: Cambridge University Press.

NOTES

1. The International Social Survey Programme (ISSP) conducted the Citizenship 2004 module in all 41 of its member nations in 2004. The General Social

Survey conducted the ISSP Citizenship module in the United States as part of a 2004 national survey. The 29 nations included in this study represent nearly all of the world's richest democracies, with democracies being defined as nations having Freedom House scores of 1 for political rights and 1 for civil liberties. GDP per capita (2004) for each nation included here ranked from 2nd to 37th globally (among democracies). Survey data from Estonia (32nd in GDP per capita among democracies), Greece (25th), Iceland (6th), Ireland (9th), Italy (20th), Lithuania (35th), Luxemburg (1st), and Malta (29th) were not available from the ISSP at the time of writing.

2. Surveys from New Zealand demonstrate a similar increase in trust in government there, up from 31 percent trusting in 1993 to 44 percent in 2005.

3. A variant of this explanation argues that media scrutiny of the regular workings of representative government reveals bargaining and partisan strategy that the public has no taste for (Hibbing & Theiss-Morse, 2001). The legitimacy of representative institutions suffers, and incentives to participate out of civic loyalty may now be weaker. A summary of corruption issues involving the 2006 U.S. Congress can be found in the report *Beyond Delay: The 20 Most Corrupt Members of Congress.* Washington, D.C.: Citizens for Responsibility and Ethics in Washington.

Index

Page numbers followed by *f* indicate figures; and those followed by *t* indicate tables.